SONJA SCHLESIN
Gandhi's South African Secretary

George Paxton

Pax Books

Published 2006

Published and distributed by
Pax Books
2/1, 87 Barrington Drive
Glasgow G4 9ES
Scotland

ISBN
0 9519022 1 0
978 0 9519022 1 9

Printed by Clydeside Press, 37 High Street, Glasgow G1 1LX

To Margaret

nihil est vicissitudine
studiorum officiorumque
iucundius
(Cicero *De Amicitia*)

'Nothing is more delightful than
the mutual exchange of zeal and service'

Preface

The personality and character of the young woman whom Gandhi regarded so highly, as revealed in his *The Story of My Experiments with Truth* and *Satyagraha in South Africa*, intrigued me for many years.

Sonja Schlesin was still a young woman when Gandhi left South Africa but she apparently did not feature in the Gandhi story after 1914. What did she do for the rest of her life ? Did she not involve herself in public affairs after the Gandhi period ?

Nothing seemed to be published specifically about her, so about eight years ago I started to search for evidence of her later life and was able to discover sufficient to publish a paper on her in 1999 (*Gandhi Marg* Vol. 21 No. 3, and later in *Jewish Affairs* Pesach 2001).

Since then a slightly fuller relating of her life has become possible, hence this short biography. It is by no means a full biography as there are periods in her later life in particular which remain hidden, but it is, I believe, still worth telling even in its far from complete form and this publication will hopefully lead others in the future to fill some of the gaps.

I owe a debt of gratitude to a number of people who corresponded with me in the early stages of my research (some of whom are now deceased). Dorothy Schlesin, whose husband was a first cousin of Sonja, was the first correspondent from South Africa; Ivan Elion of the Jewish Genealogical Society of Johannesburg; Moira Soffe Bold, a former pupil of Sonja who became Chief Medical Officer for schools in Natal; Ruth Keech who as a girl met Sonja briefly; Sita Gandhi-Dhupelia, oldest daughter of Manilal Gandhi and grand-daughter of Mohandas; Michael Imber, former Attorney-General of Natal, who met Sonja when she became a mature student after her retiral; Eric Itzkin, Curator of Cultural History at MuseuMAfricA; Sharon Farrell who is writing the history of Krugersdorp High School .

In addition I am grateful to two leading Gandhi scholars: Professor Margaret Chatterjee whom I first met through the Gandhi Foundation in London and whose book *Gandhi and His Jewish Friends* was an inspiration, and Professor James Hunt to whom I pay a special tribute as he generously provided me with information he had collected on Schlesin and also encouraged me to pursue my own research. Thanks are also due to Gopalkrishna Gandhi who, while Indian Ambassador to South Africa, pointed me in the direction of Jim Hunt.

I also wish to acknowledge the generous help of Margaret McGregor who proof-read the text, and David Gudgeon who designed the cover.

Contents

Illustrations –
Photographs on pages 57, 58 supplied by Gandhi Literature Centre, Delhi
Photographs on pages 59, 60 supplied by Sharon Farrell

I

"You keep her if you can manage her"

Mohandas Karamchand Gandhi, barrister-at-law of the Inner Temple, London, arrived in Durban, South Africa, on the *SS Safari* from Bombay on Tuesday 23 May 1893. What brought him to South Africa was the opportunity of employment. In the two years he had spent in India as a newly qualified barrister he had failed to establish himself in a proper career due to a combination of meagre knowledge of Indian law and his lack of confidence at speaking in court. When the prospect arose of a year's work as legal agent to a Gujarati merchant with business in South Africa he took it, even although it would once more mean leaving his family – wife Kasturba, 5 year old Harilal and baby Manilal – behind.

Indians, particularly Gujaratis, had been trading with east and south Africa for centuries but in more recent times Indians had been brought as indentured (contracted) labourers to the sugar plantations of Natal. After the emancipation of slaves in the British Empire in 1833, recruiting labourers became a problem for the plantation owners. Those in Mauritius began recruiting Indian 'coolies' in 1834, and those in South Africa began recruiting from India from 1860. The period of indenture was five years initially but later it was reduced to two years at the end of which they had to return home. At a later stage they were recruited for the coal mines. When Gandhi arrived in Natal there were about 50,000 Indians there as well as 50,000 whites and 400,000 blacks. Of the Indian labourers the majority came from the Madras Presidency (Tamil and Telegu speakers) and Bihar (Hindi speakers). However, initially he was concerned with the small community of merchants, mostly Gujarati Muslims, who were usually called Arabs, and who had started to arrive from 1875. Their clerks were normally Hindus or Parsis. The Europeans referred to Indians as 'coolies' or 'sammies'.

On his way to Pretoria to meet Dada Abdulah, his employer, Gandhi was ejected from the train at Pietermaritzburg because he – an Indian – was travelling First Class. This first encounter with racism – and more was to follow before he reached his destination – delivered a shock that was to have long-term repercussions, both for his future and for South Africa's.

Over the coming months the business dispute between Dada Abdulah and his cousin Tyeb Sheth, which had brought Gandhi to South Africa, was resolved by arbitration and Gandhi was then free to return home. However, he had been closely following the developing efforts of the European politicians who were trying to ensure that the Indian population of South Africa would continue indefinitely to be without political power. Instead of leaving for India in April 1894 he was asked by the Indian merchants to stay and organise resistance to the proposed legislation in Natal which was to deprive Indians of the franchise. He did not object at this time to property or income restrictions such as existed in Cape Colony but to a racial restriction. In August the Natal Indian Congress was formed to fight for the civil liberties of the Indian community with Gandhi as its secretary. They had some initial success in getting a proposed poll tax of £25 reduced to £3 although this latter was to form a central feature of campaigns in the future.

In September he was admitted as an attorney in the High Court of Natal in spite of opposition from the Natal Law Society.[1] Over the years he was to build up a successful practice and, at the same time, pursue an increasingly active life as a political activist. In June 1896 he at last sailed for India where he conducted propaganda for the South African Indian cause and then left India with his family to settle in South Africa for an unknown period. This turned out to be, in total, more than twenty years.

The family's arrival at Durban in December was eventful. Due to some misreporting of what Gandhi had written while in India many white Durban residents had determined that the immigrants would have a hostile reception and in particular when Gandhi disembarked he was attacked by a mob. Due to the courage and quick thinking of the wife of the superintendent of police, Mrs Alexander, who put her parasol up over Gandhi, he survived with only bruising and cuts.

The Gandhis' other two sons were born in the next four years, Ramdas in 1897 and Devadas in 1900. During 1899 Gandhi organised an Ambulance Corps of Indians to serve in the Anglo-Boer War, partly as an attempt to improve the standing of Indians as members of the Empire, even although his sympathies were with the Boers. The family returned to India in October 1901 and they soon settled in Bombay where Gandhi began to build a legal career, at the same time making many contacts among the politically active reformers. Visiting Bengal he observed with horror the animal sacrifices at the Kali Temple in Calcutta.

He also made a study of the Hindu reform organisation founded

by Raja Ramohan Roy in early 19th century, the Brahmo Samaj, in which the Tagore family were active. He also visited Rangoon and was impressed by the freedom and energy of Burmese women.

But once more Gandhi was called back to South Africa and arrived in December 1902. Three months later he enrolled as an attorney, this time in the Supreme Court of the Transvaal and opened an office in the centre of Johannesburg. Johannesburg had been founded only in 1886 as a mining town and had grown at an exceptional rate over the next few years until it was larger than Cape Town, which had existed for about 250 years; by the time of Gandhi's arrival Witwatersrand was producing about 30% of the world's gold.

At first he lived in a single room next to the office in Rissik Street near the courts in Government Square (now called Gandhi Square). Kasturba and the three younger boys (Harilal stayed in India for schooling) did not arrive until early in 1905 when they moved into a substantial house in the middle-class area of Troyeville – although it had to be rented as it was not permitted for a non-white to buy property there and indeed the presence of this Indian family was opposed by many residents. The Indian population of the Transvaal was only about 11,000, compared with 300,000 whites and nearly a million black Africans. The Indians were confined to certain locations, traders had to register and pay a £3 tax, and immigration into the state was strictly controlled.

In the next few years Gandhi was to develop a new method of political action which he called *satyagraha*, set up an experimental rural community at Phoenix near Durban (1904), and establish a newspaper, *Indian Opinion* (1903). He also radically changed his lifestyle in line with his evolving philosophy.

When Gandhi set up his Johannesburg office in February 1903 he naturally required clerical assistance. Most stenographers and typists in South Africa were European women and he was not sure whether any would be willing to work for an Indian, but a Miss Dick, from Scotland, was happy to do so and became a very reliable help in the office. After some time she married, to become Mrs Macdonald, and left Gandhi's employ although she did some temporary work in the future when Gandhi was in particular need. A replacement was required and one day Gandhi's friend Hermann Kallenbach brought a young woman who had been working for him, Sonja Schlesin, to the office and introduced her with these words: "This girl has been entrusted to me by her mother. She is clever and honest, but she is very mischievous and impetuous. Perhaps she is even insolent. You keep her if you can manage her. I do not place her with you for the mere pay."[2]

Kallenbach suggested a wage of only £6 per month initially although Gandhi was prepared to pay up to £20 and indeed her predecessor, Miss Dick, earned over £17. Sonja was perfectly satisfied with the low figure and refused for a while to accept more and even later received no more than £10 per month. Her response to her employer's offer of more than £6 was: "I am not here to draw a salary from you. I am here because I like to work with you and I like your ideals."

Kallenbach was an architect who had settled in South Africa in 1896 and was introduced to Gandhi in 1903 by the barrister Rahim Karim Khan, eventually becoming one of his staunchest colleagues. Kallenbach was of Jewish origin as was Schlesin, and he knew Schlesin and her family because Schlesin's uncle, Victor Rosenberg, came from the same town as Kallenbach, namely Neustadt, then in Russia and now in Lithuania.

Sonja had been born in Moscow on 6 June 1888 (the same year Gandhi went to study in Britain) to Isidor Schlesin and his wife Helena Dorothy (née Schloss). Isidor Schlesin had been born in Plungian, a small predominantly Jewish town in Lithuania. He and his wife Helena (born circa 1861 and 1862 respectively) and their daughter Sonja arrived in the Cape of Good Hope around Sonja's fourth birthday in June 1892. Isidor immediately applied for British naturalisation and in the application stated that he was residing at Oudtshoorn in the Cape and gave his occupation as ostrich feather buyer, ostrich feathers being a major export of the country at that time. Later a second daughter, Rose, was born in South Africa.

When Schlesin joined Gandhi's firm she had short, dark hair, wore long skirts, and a shirt and tie, a uniform that, it would appear, she wore for the rest of her life. She was also quite small in height. From photographs we can see she often wore a very wide-brimmed hat. It is not clear when she first appeared in Gandhi's life as Gandhi does not often give dates in his writings. He refers to Miss Schlesin as being 16 or 17 which would mean it was around 1905. We know she had matriculated at the University of the Cape of Good Hope in 1903, aged 15. He was to discover that she had exceptional speed and accuracy at shorthand.

Gandhi once said: "In South Africa, I was surrounded by Jews".[3] These included businessman Lewis W. Ritch who was a theosophist who joined Gandhi's office in 1903 and became articled in March 1904, going a year later with his wife to England to train for the bar. He did much work in the Indian cause while in Britain and on his return to South Africa in 1911 continued his commitment. He also bought Gandhi's firm from him that year. Ritch was responsible for putting Gandhi in touch with Tolstoy, whose religious writings Gandhi had been reading since he arrived in South Africa. Other supporters were William M. Vogl, a draper, and his wife, E. J. Vogl; also Gabriel Isaac, a jeweller, whose visits to Phoenix settlement were appreciated by the children to whom he told animal stories illustrated with appropriate sounds and antics. He helped to get subscriptions and advertisements for Gandhi's paper *Indian Opinion*. Much later he went to jail during the Great March in 1913. As a result of his contact with the Vogls and the Issacs, Gandhi attended services at the Johannesburg synagogue a few times but most of his Jewish friends were not observant, several were theosophists in fact, and he did not develop any great interest in Judaism. The theosophical connection was important at this stage and Ritch, along wth a non-Jew, Herbert Kitchen, founded the Johannesburg Lodge.

Most important among his Jewish colleagues, in addition to Sonja Schlesin, were Henry Polak, from Britain, who became articled to him following Ritch, and Hermann Kallenbach; none of these were practising Jews. Polak, who was initially a journalist, first became aware of Gandhi when he read the latter's letter to the press criticising the Johannesburg municipality for the poor sanitation of the Indian location where there had been an outbreak of plague in March 1904. They were first introduced by Miss Ada M. Bissicks who started a vegetarian restaurant (which, however, failed due to her lack of business sense) and this was the beginning of a life-long friendship. The restaurant, the Alexandra Tea Room which was in a grand building opposite Gandhi's office, became for the period of its existence a popular place for Gandhi and his friends to meet. Polak was influenced by the ideas of Tolstoy and also Emerson and other Transcendentalists.

One of Polak's most influential acts was giving Gandhi a copy of Ruskin's *Unto This Last* to read on the 36 hours' journey from Johannesburg to Durban in October 1904. His understanding of Ruskin's book led Gandhi to set up his first rural community at Phoenix, north of Durban.[4] He bought the farm of 100 acres with its few orange and mango trees for £1000. The farm was also close to a rural commune set up by the black African John L. Dube who edited a newspaper and established a school there. At Phoenix the residents were to live a life of cooperative manual labour and be as self-sufficient as possible. Polak left his newspaper, *The Critic*, to become sub-editor of *Indian Opinion* and settled at Phoenix for a short time until Ritch left for Britain. Apart from

Gandhi's financial support for Phoenix an old friend Dr P. J. Mehta made substantial contributions.

Henry Polak was already engaged to Millie Graham Downs who was still in Britain and waiting to come to South Africa when Henry, whom she had met at the South Place Ethical Society in London, had sufficient financial security. Gandhi however persuaded Henry to proceed with the marriage and Millie came out in December 1905. With Gandhi as best-man they went to the Registrar of European Marriages in Johannesburg. The Registrar however was suspicious since Polak was staying with Indians (Gandhi and his family) and wondered if Polak was really European. Gandhi solved the problem by going to the local Magistrate, whom he knew, and getting permission to proceed with the wedding. The couple lived with Gandhi and Kasturba for quite some time. Millie was later to write a personal memoir called *Mr Gandhi the Man* giving a very vivid picture of life with the Gandhis at that period. Henry became articled to Gandhi in 1906 and also became Secretary of the British Indian Association, an organisation founded mainly by Muslim merchants before Gandhi's arrival in South Africa.

Hermann Kallenbach was born in 1871 in Neustadt (then in Russia, now in Lithuania) but brought up in a small village near the Baltic Sea. His father was a timber merchant and the family observed Jewish customs but the six sons and one daughter were educated in German schools. Hermann became apprenticed to a carpenter in Koenigsberg and then studied architecture in Stuttgart. He did one year of military service and then finished his studies in May 1896. Physical fitness was one of his enthusiasms and he was a fine athlete and especially a skater, swimmer and cyclist. In August 1896 he left for South Africa where his uncles Henry and Simon Sacke were settled in Johannesburg. Here he began to build a very successful career as an architect. He first met Gandhi in 1903 who found him to be fond of luxury but already searching for something spiritual. He also had theosophical connections. Under Gandhi's influence Kallenbach began to change, for example, becoming a vegetarian and starting to simplify his lifestyle, although he still had tendencies to extravagance, at least by Gandhi's standards, for some years to come. Kallenbach, like Gandhi, was much influenced in these years by the religious-ethical writings of Tolstoy.

The Jews who settled in South Africa presumably were drawn there for a variety of reasons but those who came from Eastern Europe in particular often suffered discrimination or even persecution in their country of origin. The Schlesins probably emigrated from Russia as a result of an expulsion of Jews from Russian cites in 1891. Czar

Alexander II (ruled 1855-81) permitted certain classes of Jews to settle outside the Pale in, for example, St. Petersburg and Moscow. By 1900 around 9000 Jews lived in Moscow. The Pale of Settlement – to which most of the 4 million Jews of the Russian Empire were legally confined – occupied the western provinces from the Crimea in the south to close to the Baltic Sea in the north and included Poland and the Ukraine. After the relatively liberal Czar was assassinated his successor Alexander III encouraged persecution of Jews and the word 'pogrom' ('like thunder') entered the English language. Between 1881 and 1917 more than two million Jews left the Russian Empire to seek a freer life, the majority going to the USA. However, about 200,000 went to Britain, 300,000 to other parts of Europe, 100,000 to Canada, and 40,000 to South Africa, the majority of the latter coming from Lithuania. Those who settled in South Africa have tended to support liberal causes and many were also enthusiastic Zionists. Although the Jews who became Gandhi's colleagues were well educated, the majority of Jewish immigrants, like the majority of Indian immigrants, were disadvantaged and poorly educated.

Mid-1906 brought a minor crisis for the British as a 'revolt' of Zulus, known as the Bambatha Rebellion, required to be put down. It had started as a protest against taxation which resulted in the killing of a British tax collector. Gandhi's sympathies were with the Zulus but once more he felt that the Indians had a duty to support the Empire in which they lived. So again he offered a corps of stretcher-bearers, which was accepted. This time he was given the rank of sergeant-major in charge of a 20 member corps. Those the corps treated included Zulus, some of whom had been left untreated for days as Europeans would not nurse them. They had mostly been beaten and flogged by British soldiers. The first-aid given by the Indian corps was greatly appreciated by the victims in spite of being unable to understand each others' languages. The corps was only active for a month but the members received a medal for the occasion. Gandhi was strongly criticised, not for the last time, by Indian nationalists for his actions in raising a corps within the British army.

It was during his service in the corps that Gandhi took an important decision about his personal life, and that was to become celibate. Such an idea had been working on him for some time and the motivations in such matters are not always clear. One factor was that Kasturba, who had now given birth to four children, was in poor health and another pregnancy was not advisable, but her husband did not believe in artificial methods of birth control. There was also the fact that

Gandhi never got over the experience of the death of his father coinciding with Mohandas having sexual intercourse with his wife – so for him there was an element of guilt involved in all sexual relations. From that time, when husband and wife were 36, they ceased to have a sexual relationship. Whatever Kasturba thought, her husband saw it in a positive light. Another change was that he gave up his spacious house in Troyeville, settled Kasturba and the boys at Phoenix, and moved into the small house on the outskirts of town occupied by the Polaks where he stayed from August 1906 until February 1908.

II

The Birth of Satyagraha

On the political front trouble was brewing again for the Indian community. A proposed Asiatic Law Amendment Ordinance required all Indians in the Transvaal from 8 years of age to register with prints of all ten fingers. Trade licences were dependent on possession of a registration certificate. This led to the convening of a meeting, by a merchant, Hajee Ojer Ally, which was held in the Empire Theatre[5] in Johannesburg on 11 September 1906. This memorable meeting was attended by about 3000, which was a very high proportion of the adult male population of the Transvaal. During the meeting another Muslim merchant, Hajee Habib, declared that he would not submit to the Ordinance and this inspired Gandhi to propose a solemn vow of resistance. Thus began the period of passive resistance.

However he continued to put some faith in the British Government and so he went to Britain in October with Ally as fellow delegate, being met on arrival by J. H. Polak, Henry's father, and Louis Ritch. With a Liberal Government, led by Campbell-Bannerman, now in power in Britain there seemed better prospects of being listened to. In London, with the help of Dadabai Naoroji, a former Liberal MP, they saw the Secretary of State for the Colonies, Lord Elgin and the Under Secretary, Winston Churchill. Elgin announced that the Ordinance would be disallowed and Gandhi returned in December feeling he had achieved something although a Commission of Enquiry was not agreed to.

The Ordinance applied to Chinese as well as Indians and their two representatives had coincidentally travelled to London on the same boat as Gandhi and Ally. Gandhi helped them with letter drafting and back in South Africa the two communities began to cooperate.

However the Transvaal was about to become self-governing and so the new government with General Botha as Prime Minister and General Smuts as Colonial Secretary proceeded, on its very first day of sitting, to pass the Immigrants Restriction Act, known as the Black Act. Gandhi's reaction was to call upon Indians to refuse to register. The Chinese in April 1907 took an oath of resistance and Indians spoke at Chinese meetings and vice versa. *Indian Opinion* carried a special supplement on the Chinese leader Leung Quinn. Gandhi himself after refusing to register was arrested at the end of 1907 – as was Quinn and about 200 Asian resisters – and sentenced a few weeks later to two months' imprisonment – his first experience of prison. Conditions in prison were unpleasant and there was a serious risk of attack by criminal prisoners, although he did have the opportunity to read – a practice that he was to make good use of on the various occasions he was incarcerated in the future. It was at this period that the term '*satyagraha*' was adopted. Its origin was that Gandhi, finding unsatisfactory the term 'passive resistance' that was then used, announced a competition in *Indian Opinion* for a new term. A relative, Maganlal Gandhi, came up with '*sadagraha*' meaning 'firmness in a good cause'. Gandhi altered it to '*satyagraha*' or 'firmly holding to the truth'.

On New Year's Day 1908 when the Restriction Act came into force a mass rally was held in a mosque attended by about 2,500. Sonja Schlesin wanted to address the rally and had sought her parents' permission to do so. In the event Gandhi actually read her speech for her:

> *Now that the struggle has reached its culminating point, I, who have followed it with the closest attention almost from its inception, would fain say a few words of sympathy, of heartfelt sympathy, in the sufferings which you have already undergone, in the sufferings still before you, of which the former are but a foretaste. But I implore you not to flinch from the hardships which now confront you, not to falter at the shoals ahead, but to continue steadfast on your heroic resolve to give up all, aye very life itself, for the noble cause of country and religion. Let me remind you of a similar crusade now being waged by my sisters in England. I refer to the suffragettes. For the sake of a principle, they are prepared to lose their all, to brave innumerable trials. Many have already suffered imprisonment, more are ready, nay eager, to do so. If delicately nurtured women can do this, will hardy men, inured to toil, do less ? Do not swerve from the course upon which you have entered, be true to the ideal before you; and 'Heart within and God o'erhead', proceed to conquer or to die. And if you do that, if you adhere to your solemn covenant with God, if you prove yourselves resolute in deed, as you have already shown yourselves gentle in method, then it will not be to die ! Success then is assured, victory is yours, is ours.*[6]

The sentiments are very similar to those expressed by Gandhi at this time in, for example, *Indian Opinion*. He had taken a keen interest in the women's suffrage movement when in Britain in 1906 and took inspiration from it, although the later turn towards a more violent approach by the Women's Social and Political Union disappointed him. By the time of his visit to Britain in 1909 the increasing extremism of the suffrage movement had led him to warn the Indian community against going down such a path which would alienate those they wished to convince of the justice of their cause.

Smuts now agreed to reconsider the Act if Indians registered voluntarily and Gandhi took Smuts at his word and accepted this. The signatories, in addition to Smuts and Gandhi, were Quinn, Thambi Naidoo, and the editor of the *Transvaal Leader*, Albert Cartwright. Gandhi and the other *satyagrahis* were released on 31 January 1908. However the voluntary registration incensed some of the Indians and a number of Pathans led by Mir Alam Khan assaulted Gandhi, as well as Thambi Naidoo and Essop Mia (President of the British Indian Association), in the street ten days after Gandhi's release from prison when they was going to register. The assault on Gandhi was a serious one and when he recovered consciousness a clergyman, Joseph Doke, was bending over him. Doke had gone to the registry office as he feared trouble might arise and now offered to take Gandhi home where he and his wife would tend him after a doctor had been called. Gandhi was always a strong believer in 'natural' cures and to the consternation of the doctor, Gandhi requested a mud plaster and so the Dokes' son Clement was sent out to find mud. There was a vacant plot of land nearby and after removing the topsoil Clement brought home some clean mud which was put on the invalid's face.[7] When after ten days he had recovered sufficiently Gandhi moved in to Kallenbach's house called The Kraal which the latter had designed in the form of a traditional African dwelling. Here Joseph Doke often visited them while he was writing the biography of Gandhi which was to be the first of the Indian leader to be published. Gandhi had requested that his attackers not be prosecuted although this request was ignored. However, after they had been released from prison they apologised to Gandhi for misjudging him.

Shortly afterwards the Indian community, through the British Indian Association, expressed their appreciation of those of the white community who had worked for their cause, including Henry Polak who was given a gift of £50 and Schlesin and Isaac who were given £10 each. A dinner attended by about 40 Indians and 30 Europeans was also organised and attenders included the Polaks, the Vogls, the Dokes, Isaac, Kallenbach, and Schlesin. Gandhi wrote: "Miss Schlesin ... taxed herself to her utmost by labouring day and night".[8] Cartwright was also present, as was J. W. McIntyre, a Scottish theosophist articled to Gandhi. The President of the Chinese Association, Leung Quinn, was there too. William Hosken, member of the Legislative Assembly of Transvaal, spoke for the whites. Hosken, although a friend of the mine-owners was nevertheless a liberal in race relations. The Chinese community had a separate meeting in their own 'elegantly decorated' hall, as Gandhi described it, and Schlesin was given a gold watch by them also in appreciation of her support. At their meeting Gandhi was presented with an address which said:

> *It was thanks to your political acumen that this excellent settlement was effected. You were the only one who could have achieved this, and we are very grateful to you for what you have done. But for you, we would have lost. But we revere you especially for your good qualities of character, which, we believe, ennobled our campaign, with the result that Asiatic communities are treated today with respect. You combine courage with courtesy and humility, on account of which all of us bear you love and want to seek your guidance.*[9]

Unfortunately celebrations were premature as Smuts did not repeal the Act. Negotiations between Smuts and Gandhi continued over points of disagreement until in Mid-July Indians took to trading as hawkers without licenses as a protest against lack of progress. On 16 August a mass meeting at the Hamidia Mosque made a bonfire of some 800 registration certificates. Government response resulted in deportation for about 1000 Indians and 2,500 were sentenced to imprisonment. After a visit to Durban, Gandhi tried to cross into Transvaal early in October and was arrested at Volksrust along with 15 others, none of whom had registration certificates. He was sentenced to two months' imprisonment with hard labour and was set to work road making, planting trees and labouring in a cemetery. In London on 30 November at the New Reform Club, Gopal Krishna Gokhale, distinguished leader of the Indian National Congress, spoke on the South African Indians' treatment as contributing to his loss of faith in British rule. Gandhi was released on 12 December and after meetings in Transvaal he went to Phoenix to see Kasturba who was ill. Harilal Gandhi was arrested, not for the first time, as a prohibited immigrant. Harilal had married in India without his parents' permission and to their disappointment, but he and his wife had arrived at Phoenix early in 1907 and Harilal soon took an active part in *satyagraha*. Kasturba was operated upon early in the new year (1909) and remained seriously ill for three months. Gandhi was once more arrested on his way to Johannesburg on 15 January but released. *Satyagraha* continued and on 25 February Gandhi and Polak were sentenced to three months' imprisonment. Gandhi was transferred from Volksrust Gaol to Pretoria Central Gaol where he was put to polishing the floors and doors.

III

Aspiring Attorney

Meanwhile, Schlesin was the stalwart of the office, but she had plans for her future career. Ritch, Polak and McIntyre had all trained in law in Gandhi's office and now Schlesin wanted to do likewise. She was indentured as a clerk on 24 February 1909 (the day before Gandhi's arrest) supported by her father, Isidor, as her legal guardian. The Articles of Clerkship were witnessed by Gandhi, Polak, and McIntyre as well as Schlesin herself and her father. The training was to last three years.

However, on the 26 April 1909 *The Transvaal Leader* reported thus:

> *An application was made by Mr Liechtenstein before Mr Justice Bristowe in the High Court, Pretoria, on Friday afternoon, on behalf of a young lady named Sonja Schlesin, for an order of the Court impelling the Transvaal Law Society to register her articles of clerkship as an attorney's clerk. Mr Justice Bristowe refused the application, with costs, and declined to depart from the universal practice, which precluded the admission of ladies as attorneys. Miss Schlesin is of Russian birth, and desired the registration of her articles as a clerk with Mr M. K. Gandhi of Johannesburg." The exact wording of the refusal was: "... the articling of women is entirely without precedent in South Africa and was never contemplated by the law..."* [10]

It would appear that this was the first application by a woman in South Africa.

The entry of women to the professions – other than teaching and nursing – was one that began slowly in the second half of the 19th century. In general the USA seems to have led the way and medicine was the first field in which women became established. Elizabeth Blackwell was the first woman graduate in medicine, in New York in 1849, and she later settled in Britain where she had a long career. Elizabeth Garrett Anderson received her medical licence in Britain in 1865, and in France the first woman graduated in 1875, closely followed by the first Russian at St Petersburg in 1877. Maria Montessori, later famed for her educational work, graduated in medicine in Italy in 1896. Gandhi was to visit her school in London in 1931 and meet her there.

In pure science, Marie Curie dominated the field. Born Marya Sklodowska in Warsaw, she settled in France, married the equally distinguished physicist Pierre Curie, and was on the Faculty of the Ecole Normale Supérieure in 1900. In 1903 she was awarded the Nobel Prize for Physics jointly with her husband, and eight years later a second Nobel Prize in Chemistry, the first person to receive two. In Britain it was not until 1945 that chemists Kathleen Lonsdale and Marjorie Stephenson were elected to the Royal Society.

The first woman to practice at the American Bar was Arabella Mansfield in 1869, but it was not until 1919 that a woman was accepted by an English Inn of Court. This was Helena Normanton who practised in the High Court from 1922 and became the first woman King's Counsel. The first woman to take a law degree in Britain was the Indian Cornelia Sorabji (1866-1954), who was a Parsi, graduating in law from Oxford in 1892 and later practising at the bar in India and in England. It was in 1923 that legislation was passed in South Africa permitting women to practice law there. By that time Gandhi had long gone from South Africa and Schlesin had settled into teaching, but as we shall see later she was still attracted to law, even in old age.

Gandhi himself was to give up the practice of law in the later stages of the South African struggle and he never took up practice when he settled in India, although his legal experience proved invaluable in his work for Indian independence.

IV

The Struggle Continues

Millie Polak had started an organisation for Indian women, the Transvaal Indian Women's Association, and in March 1909 Schlesin became its secretary. The other leading figure in the organisation was Mrs E. J. Vogl who ran classes for the Indian women and organised bazaars. Ideally, Indian women would have taken the initiative but their lack of education made this difficult. Gandhi observed in *Indian Opinion*:

> *Miss Schlesin, while in love with her work, is not in love with the official position she occupies. She considers that the office should rightly belong to an Indian [...] Miss Schlesin, like the male European workers in South Africa for the Indian cause, demonstrates the unity of human nature, whether residing in a brown-skinned or a white-skinned body, and also that South Africa is not devoid of disinterested souls.*[11]

Schlesin was invaluable on the organisational side not only of the law practice but of the *satyagraha* campaign. She was responsible for the large sums of money required; she edited articles for *Indian Opinion;* she communicated with all the leaders of the movement; she visited *satyagrahis* in prison, and much more. She was reliable, hard-working and efficient; but she spoke her mind freely which did cause some trouble. As Gandhi recorded in his autobiography:

> *Some of her idiosyncrasies were at times too much for Mr Kallenbach and me ... She seemed to mind neither age nor experience. She would not hesitate even to the point of insulting a man and telling him to his face what she thought of him. Her impetuosity often landed me in difficulties, but her open and guileless temperament removed them as soon as they were created.*[12]

After another spell in prison Gandhi decided to go to London in the summer of 1909 to try to influence British politicians with the help particularly of Lord Ampthill, the former Viceroy of India. He had little expectations himself and it was more to satisfy other elements of the Indian community at the time. Two deputations, consisting of four persons each, were to go to London and to India respectively, the former led by Gandhi and the latter included Polak. However, some of the delegates were arrested before their departure and the result was that only Gandhi and Hajee Habib proceeded to Cape Town for departure to Britain, while Polak went alone to India. While they were at sea, an India Office official, Sir William Curzon-Wyllie, was shot by a twenty-two year old student, Madan Lal Dhingra, at a reception of the National Indian Association in London. Among the younger generation in India there was a growing belief that violence against the Raj would be necessary to end British rule and this prospect was to greatly exercise Gandhi's mind at this time.

In his contacts with Lord Morley, Secretary of State for India, and Lord Ampthill, Gandhi emphasised the very different approaches of the *satyagrahis* and the Indian advocates of violence. However, on 24 October he attended a dinner organised by the extremists and was one of the speakers. On the opposing side was 26 year old Vinayak Savarkar. They both spoke symbolically using the epic *Ramayana* to talk of different means of overcoming injustice and oppression.

On 29 July Gandhi attended a suffragette meeting in St James's Hall. He had been aware of the women's suffrage movement for some years and indeed his use of direct action was influenced by them. At a mass meeting in St James's Hall on 29 July, held to present the hunger-strikers who had briefly been imprisoned, he met Emmeline Pankhurst, leader of the Women's Social and Political Union, and also Emmeline Pethick-Lawrence who chaired the meeting. Shortly afterwards however some of the women resorted to stone-throwing, a change of tactic that Gandhi did not like. It also split the women's movement and a moderate group formed under Charlotte French Despard called the Women's Freedom League. He was impressed particularly by the latter's four months long vigil outside Parliament.

Gandhi kept in touch with Polak in India and requested Gokhale's help in the cause. Polak said of Gokhale: "Wonderful man, has most accurate knowledge of facts and principles. Huge admirer of yours." At a Congress session in Lahore, Gokhale had said of Gandhi:

> *It is one of the privileges of my life that I know Mr Gandhi personally; and I can tell you that a purer, a nobler, a braver and a more exalted spirit has never moved on this earth. He is a man who may well be described as a man among men, a hero among heroes, a patriot among patriots, and we*

may well say that in him Indian humanity at the present time has really reached its high watermark. [13]

Gandhi also asked Polak at this time to cancel Gandhi's life insurance policy while in India. He had taken it out earlier when he realised that if he had died his family would be destitute because he had given away his wife's gold jewellery. But he now considered that this showed a lack of faith. He also wrote to Tolstoy about both *satyagraha* and Tolstoy's *Letter to a Hindu*.

On 25 October the third reading of the Indian Immigration Amendment Bill passed in the Natal Legislative Assembly. After farewell meetings emphasising the need for continuing the struggle, he and Habib left for South Africa on 13 November. He also issued an invitation to Gokhale to visit South Africa. On board ship he did not rest but wrote, at great speed and using both hands, a small book, *Hind Swaraj* or *Home Rule,* which in dialogue form expounded his views on modern civilisation, views which were becoming increasingly critical and even extreme. He was now beginning to turn away from modern, European culture and develop a greater interest in Indian culture which he believed in essence was superior although it required reform and the discarding of undesirable practices.

Gandhi and Habib arrived in Johannesburg in early November where public meetings were addressed. All the time Gandhi had been in London, Schlesin was in charge of his affairs and he kept her informed of developments. In early December Gandhi addressed a women's meeting which was chaired by Mrs Vogl. It was attended mainly by Tamil women who supported *satyagraha* and whose husbands and sons had been in many cases imprisoned. Phoenix Settlement was at this time in some financial difficulties and Schlesin was appointed one of the trustees. At the beginning of 1910 *Indian Opinion* was reduced in size to cut expenses. All Gandhi's earnings were going to the paper and to the upkeep of Phoenix; Gandhi and his family were actually being financially supported by Kallenbach. In addition nearly £4000 was sent from India through Gokhale to the Satyagraha Fund.

Gandhi again wrote to Tolstoy, sending him a copy of *Indian Home Rule* for comment and Tolstoy replied that he regarded the new technique of *satyagraha* to be of the greatest importance for all humanity. On the 30 May, Kallenbach offered to the movement a farm of 1100 acres south-west of Johannesburg with extensive orchards which, with Tolstoy's permission, they named Tolstoy Farm and he and Gandhi immediately moved there. A school was established with Gandhi in charge and Kallenbach taught carpentry and sandal-making, the latter skill being learned from Trappist monks at Marianhill. Gandhi began to travel Third Class at this time to save money for the cause. On 20 November the great writer, who had been one of Gandhi's most important influences, died. In tribute he spoke on Tolstoy and his ideas at the Socialist Hall in Johannesburg.

The year 1911 began with the announcement in India that the Legislative Council at Calcutta would prohibit further emigration of indentured Indians to Natal. Gokhale expressed gratitude. In South Africa the Immigrants Restriction Bill received its first reading on 2 March and a period of protest and also negotiations with Smuts began. A new poll tax bill also aroused objections. In April Smuts agreed to assurances demanded by the Indian community in return for the suspension of *satyagraha*.

Around this time an American suffragette, Mrs Carrie Chapman Catt, visited Johannesburg and invited Gandhi to call at her hotel which was in Permanent Buildings, the first building in Johannesburg to have a lift installed. She recalled later:

> *At the hour named a pretty, intelligent young Russian Jewess called and explained that she was Mr Gandhi's secretary and that no Indian was permitted to enter a hotel to call upon a guest. A prominent lawyer to whom I told the tale offered the use of his office for the purpose of an interview, so again I wrote, stating the time and place when I would be glad to receive him. Again the pretty little Jewess came to the lawyer's office to say that Mr Gandhi had come but the elevator operator refused to take him up and he would not so far demean himself as to walk when the European was carried. This challenged my curiosity and I told the young girl to tell him to go back to his office and that I would call upon him. Directly Miss Cameron and I, escorted by the secretary, were on our way. She took us into quarters apparently occupied exclusively by Indians [...] We found the man seated behind an American desk – a small very black man with his head wrapped in a very white turban.*[14]

Ritch started legal practice in Gandhi's office in April. At this time Schlesin, as independently minded as ever, wrote the following playful note to Gandhi (using the archaic word 'wot' for 'know'):

> *Your typewriting grows more beautiful daily. You say that 'Necessity is the mother of invention' and, therefore, you are doing your own typing. What you mean is that 'Necessity knows no law' and, therefore, you have*

taken upon yourself to disregard the anti-machinery injunction laid down in a certain booklet we wot of. [15]

The booklet referred to was none other than *Hind Swaraj.*

In January there was a games day at the Farm for the roughly 20 boys and girls in residence at which Schlesin assisted with the running, jumping, tug-of-war and other games at which prizes were given. In January she also passed an Intermediate Arts Examination at the University of the Cape of Good Hope and by August was intending to take up a teaching appointment (perhaps a requirement for a teaching certificate) and hoping that she would be assigned to a 'coloured' school. During September she taught in a government school in Mayfair.

In August Kallenbach, on a visit to Europe, saw Schlesin's uncle Dr Max Rosenberg and his wife in Tauroggen and they wanted to know everything about her – "I was not too flattering", said Kallenbach who always seemed to find her style more difficult to stomach than did Gandhi.

The same month further trouble arose when Indian merchants looked as if they would lose their rights of ownership in Krugersdorp. Ritch declared he would be prepared to go to prison in defence of their rights. More trouble came in November when the Government announced that the £3 poll tax on re-indentured Indians would not be abolished as previously promised. It seems that Schlesin may have left the office, now sold to Ritch, for a period as Kallenbach asks in a letter to Gandhi in response to hearing that Schlesin is returning on 1 October: "Could she not get on with Ritch ?" Schlesin and her sister Rose were at Tolstoy Farm over Christmas that year. It seems they more often came for one day.

Schlesin had a minor clash with authority during her period as Secretary of the Transvaal Indian Women's Association (1911-12). While travelling Third Class on the railways on two occasions she was asked, in a reverse of Gandhi's early experience, to move to carriages assigned to whites. She refused and followed this up by challenging the railway administration to prosecute her. Gandhi defended her stance in *Indian Opinion* in August 1912 and published the correspondence between Schlesin and the Railway Administration. He commented:

The question raised by Miss Schlesin is undoubtedly one of very great delicacy, and requires on her part a great deal of tact and carefulness. It is equally necessary, on the part of the Administration, to use tact and discretion. We consider that, in her capacity as Honorary Secretary of the Indian Women's Association, Miss Schlesin could take up no other position, consistently with her dignity and with the interests that are under her charge. She could not properly leave her co-workers, who are travelling with her in a common mission and separate herself from them during the railway journey. That would be carrying too far the doctrine of concession to popular prejudice, unreasonable and unreasoned as it is ... [16]

On 22 October Gokhale, whom Gandhi held in great respect, arrived in Cape Town from Britain and travelled by train to Johannesburg where he was welcomed by a specially built arch designed by Kallenbach. A vegetarian dinner was held in Johannesburg for more than 300 Indians and Europeans, the first such mixed eating in a public place. Throughout the five week tour Gokhale was accompanied by Gandhi. After public meetings they proceeded to Tolstoy Farm on 2 November for two days of rest. On 8 November there was a reception at the Town hall in Durban; on 11 November Gokhale paid a visit to Phoenix, and on 14 November he had an interview with Botha and Smuts. During his stay he was able to observe Schlesin at work and paid this tribute to her:

I have rarely come across such purity, single-minded devotion to work and great determination as I have seen in Miss Schlesin. I was simply astonished how she had sacrificed her all for the Indian cause without expecting any reward whatever. And when you add to all this her great ability and energy, these qualities combine to make her a priceless asset to your movement. I need hardly say it and yet I say that you must cherish her. [17]

Gokhale left South Africa optimistic about the prospects for the Indian community, having taken the whites at their word. In India the Indian National Congress passed a resolution on 28 December demanding the total abolition of indenture.

This year saw further personal changes for Gandhi as he gave up the wearing of European dress. He also ceased taking milk, along with Kallenbach at the latter's suggestion, and restricted his diet to fruits and nuts.

1913 saw the climax of the struggle. In January, Tolstoy Farm was closed down and the *satyagraha* centre moved to Phoenix. When a decision of the Supreme Court (the Searle judgement) effectively made non-Christian marriages illegal and wives and children of Indian men resident in South Africa unable to enter the country, women began to involve themselves in *satyagraha*. In April, Kasturba expressed her wish to join those courting arrest. On 4 May, Schlesin, as Secretary of the Transvaal Indian Women's Association, cabled the Minister of the Interior expressing the women's intention to offer *satyagraha*. A letter from Gandhi to Gokhale in June reveals that Schlesin continues to do "all the public work in Johannesburg but for her maintenance works elsewhere." The Immigration Regulation Bill and the Amendment Bill including the £3 tax proceeded through legislative assemblies. On 15 September, with negotiations and representations having no effect, *satyagraha* was resumed. Twelve men, including Manilal and Ramdas, and four women, including Kasturba, left Durban for Volksrust by train to cross the border, Volksrust being just inside Transvaaal. They were arrested and sentenced to three months' hard labour. Gandhi then left Durban for Johannesburg calling at Pietermaritzburg and Ladysmith to gather support and at Ladysmith he refused to leave his train compartment which was reserved for Europeans. Small-scale disobedience continued with Manilal Gandhi and some women arrested.

On 17 October Gandhi visited the Natal coalfields near Newcastle and urged indentured Indians to strike until repeal of the £3 tax was promised. Seventy-eight workers went on strike initially and this built up to more than 3,000. By 23 October nine coal mines were closed and on 28 October Gandhi led 1700 *satyagrahis* from Newcastle; by the end of the month 300 *satyagrahis* were in prison. The march known as The Great March left Charleston on 6 November for Volksrust and consisted of 2,037 men, 127 women and 57 children. Gandhi, Polak and Kallenbach were arrested (Gandhi received a nine months' sentence) and the marchers were deported by special train to Natal. Schlesin stayed at Charlestown looking after the remaining women and children and the elderly. Kallenbach had been arrested while he and Schlesin had been discussing plans on the Charlestown station platform. While he was held in Volksrust prison Schlesin visited him almost daily to discuss organisational details. Schlesin was never at any time arrested, although she would have liked to be, but did not court arrest as she was considered to be more useful coordinating matters from outside.

Plantation Indians now went on strike and the total from different areas of production reached about 50,000. Military police brought in fired on workers with many being wounded and some killed. On 30 November mass meetings were held in Durban, Johannesburg and Pietermaritzburg. Gokhale now cabled Gandhi that two English clergymen, C. F. Andrews and W. W. Pearson, would visit South Africa to inquire into the conditions of the Indians. Gandhi, Polak and Kallenbach did not serve their full sentences and were released on 18 December as a Commission of Enquiry started and three days later Gandhi spoke at a mass meeting in Durban dressed as an indentured Indian and announced his intention of eating only one meal per day as mourning for those Indians who had been killed during the struggle.

We have a vivid picture of Schlesin around this time in her teaching role from Prabhudas Gandhi, son of Chhaganlal Gandhi who was one of Gandhi's cousins. He remembered her at Phoenix in 1913 when he was 12 years old.

When Bapuji was arrested and sentenced to one year's imprisonment, a white girl arrived about 15 days later. She had bobbed hair, a white shirt and black skirt reaching her knees. I had seen many white girls, but this girl coming to Phoenix was more impressive. Her dress was quite simple, and her face was serious. She talked to Magankaka [Maganlal Gandhi] *with a face full of worry but after that she laughed again and again. When she laughed her cheeks had dimples which attracted one and all. I have seldom found elsewhere such laughing, very fresh and so incessant. I asked Devdaskaka* [Devadas Gandhi] *about the girl. He said, "She is Miss Schlesin'.*

On hearing her name I lost all strangeness, and awakened faith in her. I had been eager to see Miss Sonja Schlesin for years. I had heard about her cleverness and alertness from the people who had come from the farm to join Phoenix. She was an educated and clever girl. When Bapuji was a practising pleader, she wrote for long hours and yet she was never tired. In short-hand she was the best in South Africa.

She was clever and playful as well as mischievous. She carried out Bapuji's work without stopping and at the same time she vexed him. Her jesting nature was known to Gandhiji. One of the incidents during Bapuji's practice was well-known among us. She was not addicted to smoking, but one day for pleasure's sake she lighted a cigarette and started smoking in the face of Bapuji. She sent a cloud of smoke on his face. Bapuji did not say anything. He slapped her twice. The slap echoed in the office in front of the white assistants. They all knew how Bapuji recruited both Indians and Europeans. Miss Schlesin was too bold, but she learned the limitations of playfulness. He did not slap her to avenge an insult. She was like a daughter to Bapuji, so he would not tolerate any digression on her part. How could such a pure girl touch a cigarette ? Also, her joking could not be of the wrong type ! With this attitude Bapuji punished her as he would punish me or Devdaskaka, and she tolerated slapping with the same attitude. After that incident she progressed greatly in Bapuji's company.

In addition to this, I had heard many incidents about Miss Schlesin from the residents of Tolstoy Farm. Whenever I heard about her, I longed to see her in Phoenix and witness her jocular nature. Bapuji has spoken volumes about Miss Schlesin in his History of Satyagraha in South Africa. Even though he has praised her highly, he was restrained in doing so. He could have described her greatness in higher terms.

The initial business between Miss Schlesin and Magankaka came to an end and we finished our meals. We heard their talk. Miss Schlesin had accompanied the 4000 strikers' march from Charlestown. She continued doing so until Bapuji, Mr Polak and Mr Kallenbach and other strikers were arrested and accommodated. After that she came to Phoenix under Bapuji's instruction. I was habituated to listen and see. I could not talk much. Others would ask her many questions and they got unfailing replies.

Some 20 years ago from today ladies with bobbed hair were rare. Somebody asked Miss Schlesin, "Why don't you have long hair ?" She immediately replied, "Why waste time in fixing it ? Should only males be allowed to remain free from that ? Should all rights be reserved for men ?" During her conversation this sentence was often repeated. Really no man could defeat her or weaken her ideas. She had full discretion of her energy at work. Even in the dark of night she would run to the railway station. She could successfully vie with any clever man in respect of writing, doing any work, managing affairs, issuing orders and finding solutions to all possible problems. She assisted Magankaka in writing in Indian Opinion columns which were ready in the printing process.

She could not stay long at Phoenix as she had to provide help to the strikers. For this she had to move between Natal and the Transvaal, running here and there until the end of the campaign. She became our constant companion from her first visit to Phoenix. With the passage of time she became the head of our school. She taught us much, especially myself. She taught me to write essays and not be afraid of English spelling, but I will describe those incidents in the chapters that follow. Here it will suffice to say that her arrival at Phoenix removed its emptiness to a great extent.

There was another younger girl in Phoenix. There was less of sweetness in her voice. [...] In other matters that girl was playful, pleasant and sweet talking. But during her informal talks Miss Schlesin once stated that she had a dislike for that girl at sight. She also added that until that time she

never had any dislike for any child and so she used to keep her by her side more and more. And I must state that she really taught that girl sincerely. Not only that she looked after her body, even though she had her mother and sister. Generally she was not in the habit of placing the child in her lap, but she used to place that girl in her lap and took care about her hair and face. It was a great spiritual endeavour on her part to develop reverence for human beings.

[...]

In our school there was no tradition of giving prizes to students. Bapuji used to give marks, but if we entered into counting mutual superiority he did not like it, rather he condemned it. His marking process spelt our progress, that is we could ourselves detect our progress whether we had improved today over yesterday. He insisted that we should check our progress and make more attempts for betterment. He did not like mutual competition at all. But Miss Schlesin was of an independent nature. She did not believe in following Bapuji literally. Bapuji also gave her much liberty. So she arranged to award prizes for competition even against Bapuji's policy. She demanded essays not only from the students but also from the workers of Phoenix. She divided the young and old residents of Phoenix into three categories and fixed prizes for all the categories separately. She arranged a special programme for reading these essays in public and appointed a committee for judging the quality of the essays presented.[18]

It is not generally noted that Gandhi promoted football matches between groups of *satyagrahis*. A Rangers Football Club had been formed in 1889 by miners originally from Glasgow and Newcastle and matches were held at their ground by *satyagrahis* between 1911 and 1913. Itzkin's *Gandhi's Johannesburg* has a photograph of Pretoria Passive Resisters and Johannesburg Passive Resisters at the Rangers ground with both Gandhi and Schlesin also present; Schlesin being the only woman among 48 men.

On 2 January 1914 Andrews and Pearson arrived in Durban and were given a reception by Gandhi. However a European workers' strike had broken out in the coal mines and this developed into a general strike with the railways and gold mines involved. Smuts acted by declaring martial law on 14 January just before Andrews and Gandhi met Smuts in Pretoria where they assured him that the *satyagrahis* would not push their position at that time of difficulty for the Government. This broke the deadlock with the Indians. After further negotiations a provisional settlement was reached on 22 January, resistance was suspended and Gandhi went off to Phoenix. Public meetings endorsed the terms and the Government released those in prison.

Gandhi now began to turn his mind to preparations for leaving South Africa for the last time, but Kasturba was seriously ill and was to remain so for some months.

On the 28 May the Bill was published. It restored the positions of Asian marriages, abolished the £3 tax and the need for registration, and the system of indenture was to end by 1920. Gandhi proposed some changes which were accepted although there were still some immigration constraints into South Africa and between the states. On 26 June the Indian Relief Act was passed, thus ending the eight years' struggle.

During his years in South Africa Gandhi had demonstrated the effectiveness of a new method of principled political action and had also welded together a diverse group of people - speaking different languages, professing different religious beliefs, and having different social status (although some Christian Indians and Tamils did not join the campaigns). And though he did not involve the majority populace at all the memory of the campaigns did have some influence on the future history of South Africa.

On 15 July Gandhi spoke at the unveiling of two memorial stones in Braamfontein Cemetery to two young victims of the struggle and Schlesin was also present. Swami Nagappen had died, aged 18, in 1909 after release from prison to which he had been sent for hawking without a licence, and Valliamma Munusamy was only 17 when she died shortly after release in 1914.

Gandhi and Kasturba, with Kallenbach, left for Britain, hoping to see Gokhale who was on his way there because of his health. Before departure they attended farewell dinners in Durban, Johannesburg and Cape Town at which Schlesin was also given addresses and presented with books. Gandhi played a glowing tribute to Schlesin for her work in the Indian cause. To his fellow Indians he recommended that they push forward with demands for full equality reminding them that truthfulness, courage and unity were required for success.

He entrusted a pair of sandals, which he had made in prison, to Polak and Schlesin to be given to Smuts. Smuts was to wear the sandals every summer at his farm near Pretoria. But at the time of Gandhi's departure Smuts expressed his relief that "the saint has left our shores, hopefully for the last time". For Gandhi's colleagues their feelings were rather different. Those of Millie Polak were probably shared by others: "As I watched the boat steam out I felt an intolerable sense of blankness come into my life. A chapter filled with movement and intensity and emotion had definitely closed."

The passengers, now travelling third class in contrast to earlier visits to Britain, arrived in London on 6 August, two days after the Great War began. There was a reception in the Hotel Cecil, near Trafalgar Square, organised by British and Indian friends including Lala Lajput Rai, Mohammed Ali Jinnah, Charlotte Despard, Albert Cartwright and Sarojini Naidu, whom he met for the first time, Sadly, Kallenbach as an Enemy Alien had to register as such and from 1915-17 was detained on the Isle of Man. Gandhi wrote often to his friend during his internment and recommended a reading list that included *The Imitation of Christ* by Thomas à Kempis, an interesting choice for a Hindu to a Jew. His goods were sent on to India as it was expected that he would come eventually but in fact Kallenbach returned to South Africa when freed.

Gandhi did not rest when in London in spite of his own poor health at this time but once more organised an Indian Volunteer Corps of students for service at the western front. At the same time some of the Phoenix settlers led by Chhaganlal Gandhi set out from South Africa to India going at first to Tagore's Shantiniketan, which they found to be less austere than the Phoenix and Tolstoy settlements and where more emphasis was put on education and the arts. Gokhale and Gandhi had many talks together before the former left London in October but little is recorded. Gandhi met Florence Winterbottom of the Ethical Society whom he had known since 1906, and the classical scholar, and later President of the Ethical Society, Gilbert Murray, who wrote of Gandhi in a perceptive essay published in *The Hibbert Journal*. In December, after a not altogether happy stay in London, which included ill-health, Gandhi and Kasturba left for India arriving at Bombay on 9 January 1915.

V

Their paths diverge

The last few years in South Africa had been a period of intense public activity for Gandhi and his associates. Gandhi had now become something of a public figure, known to those politically active in India. His views and lifestyle had changed substantially. He moved from being a constitutional reformer to a nonviolent direct actionist; he had greatly simplified his lifestyle, and that of his family, and had adopted celibacy. Although his future career was not clear it would surely involve public work and it is clear that Gandhi saw Schlesin as part of that. However it was not to be; Schlesin never went to India and remained in South Africa for the rest of her life.

Gandhi took Gokhale's advice to get to know India by travelling around the country. He was in Santiniketan in Bengal with Charlie Andrews when he received the news of Gokhale's death in Poona on 19 February 1915 and immediately travelled there. Gandhi did not however succeed Gokhale as leader of the Servants of India Society as some of the members had doubts about his suitability.

In May he set up Satyagraha Ashram at Kochrab near Ahmedabad where thirteen families from Phoenix formed the core. The rules of discipline were even stricter than those in South Africa and Andrews criticised this aspect, especially the celibacy rule. An untouchable family was soon to be admitted causing upsets within and outwith the ashram.

A letter from Gandhi at Satyagraha Ashram to Schlesin in January 1916 begins:

> *My dear daughter, You have at last favoured me with a letter. Even six letters in a year you do not call a brilliant performance. Do you ? However I must be content with what you may give me.*
>
> *You might at least have given me the credit for uttering no such nonsense as Mrs Besant's correspondent attributed to me. Natarajan* [Editor of *Indian Social Reformer*] *apologised for reproducing the calumny. What I did say bore a totally different construction. I made use of a Gujarati proverb in defence of my proposition that man continually did an injustice to woman by using her for his lusts.*[19]

Disagreements and disappointments form a strand throughout their subsequent correspondence over the next thirty years.

The following year in a talk to teachers at the National School at Ahmedabad which he founded he said:

English should be an optional subject. One should know good, at any rate correct, English. It would be excellent if we could get an English teacher for the purpose, but I can think of no one at present except Miss Schlesin. If only she would come, we could want nothing better. She is a very capable person.[20]

In August he wrote to his son Ramdas:

Tell Miss Schlesin to write to me. I am awaiting her arrival. Tell her also that there are some ten letters from me she has not answered.[21]

During 1916 the Polaks, including son Waldo (who was named after Ralph Waldo Emerson), went to India but they then settled in Britain. Thus Gandhi no longer had the company of his three closest South African colleagues – Hermann Kallenbach, Henry Polak, Sonja Schlesin.

In 1917 Gandhi was drawn into his first public campaign in India helping the indigo growers of Champaran. It was also the year he met Mahadev Desai who was to become his devoted and very efficient principal secretary – a worthy but less troublesome successor to Schlesin. In 1918 Gandhi led a *satyagraha* campaign of mill workers in Ahmedabad and then another among peasants in Kheda.

In June 1918, during his period of recruitment for the British army [22], he replied to Schlesin:

The long expected letter has come. We have all been looking forward to a letter from you.

Of course Phoenix is not going to be sold. You can have 5 acres of ground in the centre. I like your dream specially as it includes a visit to India.

It delights me to find you getting tired of the typewriter...

I have not asked Ramdas to become a tailor; not that there is no poetry in tailoring. Ramdas may become a living Sartor Resartus. But he is a conscientious boy. He wants to gain all kinds of experiences. If he becomes a poet he will be one not of words and in words, but of actions and in actions. Ramdas is a visionary. And I like visionaries. I hope you will guide him, and befriend him. I wish you would live with Manilal [at Phoenix] for a while. You could carry on your studies there.

How are the Vogls, the Phillipses, and the Dokes ? Do you ever meet them ? Where is MacIntyre ? What do you think of the community ? Do you meet Thumbi ? What has come over him ? These are questions which I should expect discussed in your letters. But something is better than nothing.

My life has become very complex. You must have read at least my important public letters. Now I am entering upon a big recruiting campaign. My work has involved constant railway travelling. I am longing for solitude and rest. They may never be my lot. Mrs Gandhi has developed remarkably. She has beautifully resigned herself to things she used to fight. But I must not describe things. You must see them for yourself.

With love, M.K.Gandhi [23]

During 1918 Schlesin registered at the University College of Johannesburg.

That summer Gandhi faced a personal crisis. He developed dysentery and was depressed. Whether conflicts in his mind over the (unsuccessful) recruiting campaign were primarily responsible or whether, as he claimed, it was due to diet, he was in a serious condition. As he began to improve slightly the family suffered a grievous blow. In October, Harilal's three year old son died of the influenza epidemic that was sweeping the world, and then only a few days later Harilal's wife Gulab died likewise. Gandhi's own condition deteriorated. Eventually Kasturba persuaded him to go to Bombay to consult a physician. The doctor insisted that his patient must start taking milk as he was extremely weak, but Gandhi's vow forbad it. Then Kasturba came up with the solution: the vow concerned cows' milk but he could surely take goats' milk. Her husband allowed himself to be persuaded and take his first glass and from then he began to recover. He regarded this decision nevertheless as a moral weakness but he took goats' milk regularly from then on.

As the Rowlatt Act permitting detention without trial was about to come into force, Gandhi wrote on 23 February 1919 a reply to a letter from Schlesin, beginning teasingly –

It was so good of you to give me credit if only for once for being business-like. My own opinion of myself is that I am the most business-like man upon the earth and, so long as no one can disillusion me, I shall continue to derive pleasure from the belief and to have a stray certificate from you only adds to the pleasure. I present you another illustration of my business-likeness. I know I would wound your vanity, self-esteem, glorious womanliness, whatever you like to call it, by making friend my carrier instead of a bank, for this very simple purpose of lending you money. Had I taken your impractical advice, it would have taken me much longer to send you the money because you must know that I am living in India where we do things in a fairly leisurely manner befitting the climate and the surroundings. Here bankers are not the servants of their clients but their masters except when the clients happen to belong to the ruling race and probably it would have cost you £15 to send £50. You with your poetic instinct set no value on money, whereas I, a simple prosaic business-like man, realise that it requires £150 to finish the education of someone. Therefore, if I spend away £15, I waste one-tenth of that sum if I can avoid having to spend it. Q.E.D.

You shall certainly treat what you have received as a loan. I believe I have already told Mr Rustomji as much but I cannot swear as I cannot keep copies of my correspondence as a rule and I shall accept repayment whenever you choose to send it, with compound interest if you will, provided that you do not borrow to pay me. You will infer from what has preceded that my health is better. I am still bed-ridden. My head is supposed to be weak and I may not undertake any great exertion. But the feel is all right and I am cheerful.

Devibehn [Ada West sister of Albert West] *writes to me regularly and tells me that you rarely [do so]. That is not how people treat their goddesses, or had women the privilege of acting different ?*

Yes, Harilal has been sorely stricken. Chanchi [Gulab] *was far superior to me. I did not specially write to you as I felt my cable to Ramdas in reply to his was enough for all. At the time, moreover, I was too ill to think of writing to anybody. All Harilal's children are here and are playing about me while I am dictating this letter.*

Passive resistance is on the topics regarding certain legislation that the Government of India are passing through the Council. The war council meets tomorrow at the Ashram. You may depend upon it that it won't be a bad copy of similar councils in which you were both an actor (or actress ?) and a fairly intelligent spectatress. You won't therefore need from me a description of the council meeting.

I am surprised at your remark about Ashrams here prohibiting the entry of women. It betrays your lack of interest in the Ashram. We have so many women here at the Ashram. We are educating them all, including three girls. The latter are no doubt our own girls. but that is not our limitation.

It is due to the disinclination of the people to send their girls under the conditions that we impose. It will delight your heart to see the transformation that the women undergo here after a few days' stay. The purdah and all other unnatural restraints fall away as if by magic. I know you will hug most of them when you come here. Only you will have to revive your knowledge of Gujarati.[24]

Schlesin must have required a loan as she was a full time student at this period. The day after he dictated this letter Gandhi notified the Viceroy of the pledge to undertake *satyagraha* over the Rowlatt Act.

Satyagraha was suspended on 18 April after there had been outbreaks of violence and on 2 June Gandhi wrote again to Schlesin:

Ramdas advises me that you have passed your teacher's examination with some distinction. You do not want me to congratulate you, I know. I am simply anxious that you should get through your final examination, because I expect you one of these days to take your place in India. The summer months are trying enough, but the winter months give you sufficient compensation. I hope you had all you wanted without any inconvenience. You will not hesitate to come to me for more, if necessary.

He then allowed himself a brief period of nostalgia –

Satyagraha is going on merrily. Civil disobedience is expected to commence very soon. How I often wish you were here for more reasons than one ! But I must plough the lonely furrow. It often makes me sad when I think of all my helpers of South Africa. I have no Doke here. I have no Kallenbach. Don't know where he is at the present moment. [Between 1918 and 1920 Kallenbach was in Berlin and East Prussia.] *Polak in England. No counterpart of Kachalia or Sorabji. Impossible to get the second edition of Rustomji. Strange as it may appear, I feel lonelier here than in South Africa. This does not mean that I am without co-workers. But between the majority of them and me, there is not that perfect correspondence which used to exist in South Africa. I do not enjoy the same sense of security which you all gave me there. I do not know the people here; nor they, me. This is all gloomy, if I were to brood over it. But I do not. I have not the time for it. I have a few moments of leisure just now. Ramdas' letter reminds me of your existence in South Africa, and I am giving myself the momentary pleasure of sharing my innermost thoughts with you. But now no more.* [25]

We do not know her inner thoughts and whether she ever seriously thought of joining her friend in India but in 1920 she became a teacher in the High School at Krugersdorp, a small mining town to the west of Johannesburg, and there she remained for the next 23 years teaching, primarily, Latin. The school, which catered for both girls and boys, was founded in a very modest way in 1903 at a time when a concentration camp, an unfortunate consequence of the Anglo-Boer War, still existed to the north of the town. Teaching was in English but they had one Afrikaans teacher. There was always a high percentage of Jewish pupils and in the town itself a synagogue was consecrated shortly after the school opened. March 1922 saw the Rand Revolt of white miners who clashed violently with Government troops under the direction of Smuts and the school was closed temporarily.

It would appear that there were virtually no communications between Gandhi and Schlesin during the years 1919-24 but this is not surprising when she was both teaching and continuing her studies, for between 1921 and 1924 she graduated from the University of Witswatersrand with a BA and MA, both First Class. Her subjects were French, Latin, English, Logic & Psychology.

But Gandhi's mind, in spite of his busy life, still turned more than occasionally to her. In a letter to Kallenbach in September 1921:

> *I often think of Miss Schlesin but of late I have been feeling anxious about her... I do want to hear from her. In any case I would like to know of her welfare ? What is she doing ?* [26]

Kallenbach had returned to Johannesburg and taken up his career in architecture again, becoming very successful. He made business trips to Europe but not to India.

Also in September 1921 Gandhi wrote in a letter to Ramdas:

> ... *I remember Miss Schlesin every day. I believe you have not forgotten her. You should meet her even if you have to make a search for her. Her public service is such that it is never to be forgotten.* [27]

In 1924, having completed her studies, Schlesin at last wrote to Gandhi at Sabarmati – to ask for an employment reference. On 15 August he replied in the bantering style of their South African days:

> *My Dear Miss Schlesin,*
>
> *Though late in the day, your letter was most welcome. If you wanted to*

make it a model of neatness, you have failed badly. The same slovenliness, the same smudging. I can almost see your inky fingers in your letter. Here is the certificate you want. You will be entitled to accuse me of untruthfulness in that I have not certified to your slovenliness. Let me hope the new 'master' will fare better. I must refuse to plead guilty to all the charges you have noted against me. Why should I care about giving you a 'business certificate' ? But how are the mighty fallen ! Regarding the £24, I thought the draft of 150 included the amount. However I am writing to Parsee Rustomji to write off the whole balance, whatever it might be, of the £150.
My health is fair. Now you have commenced to write, will you continue ?
28

The certificate Gandhi supplied is as follows:

Miss Sonja Schlesin served me as confidential secretary in South Africa for nearly seven years and during a most important part of my public life. She was entrusted with heavy responsibilities including account-keeping, involving transactions extending to four figures at a time. She came in touch with hundreds of people belonging to different races and nationalities. During my last incarceration in South Africa, she was in sole charge of my affairs. I never once had reason to doubt her integrity or ability. Indeed, she did not work for the sake of pay but for the sake of the work itself which she loved. Her services were available to me at all times of the day. Her knowledge of shorthand and literary talents were of great assistance to me. I could not wish for a better secretary. I should like to hear that she was entrusted with a post requiring close attention, strictest honesty and ability.

Whether she was seeking an administrative post outside teaching or promotion within the teaching profession is not known but it seems she was not successful in spite of Gandhi's fine reference. A former pupil, Clem Friedman, remembered her at this time as always wearing very severe long black dresses which covered her completely from neck to ankles and wrists. Over the years she played an important role in expanding the school library and helped with other cultural activities such as concerts. [29]

1927 saw a greater exchange of letters and while bed-ridden in May Gandhi wrote to Schlesin. She must have been complaining about not getting replies because he says:

So far as my memory serves me, there is not a single letter of yours which has gone by without an acknowledgement. There are many compliments which I do not and cannot appropriate; but the one about my being a prompt correspondent, I can ever claim in spite of your different experience. For, everybody else of my acquaintance has paid me the compliment of being a prompt correspondent, that is of course comparatively to many. [30]

He goes on to mention the Christian missionary E. Stanley Jones's book *The Christ of the Indian Road* which he has hurriedly read and which Schlesin must also have read. He says he will pass her letter on to Jones. He continues:

I quite agree with you that karma and the cross may well go together. If you have followed the pages of 'Young India', you must have noticed that last year I read the New Testament every Saturday to the students of our National College. I did stumble over the words "without a cause" [St. Matthew v22; words found in the Authorised Version are omitted in later translations – Ed. CWMG], and in explaining it I simply rejected the thing as redundant. But I was agreeably surprised on turning to Moffat's and Weymouth's translations which I had by me to make the discovery that you made. In reading all religious works, I have learnt one thing. Never to take them literally, but to understand the drift and catch the drift also by means of what is to me an infallible canon of interpretation, and reject those which cannot stand the test of Truth and Ahimsa. I know that even in spite of this canon of interpretation difficulties do arise; but they are solved if one has patience and if one has a living faith in God.

He also mentions his autobiography:

The autobiography is not yet complete. Ganesan [his publisher] cannot send you a copy of the autobiography. The three parts that have been completed are in course of publication in book form. But for the present, you have to rely upon the numbers of Young India which contain the chapters to date. You may borrow the volumes from Manilal or you should wait till the three parts are published in book form. You may know that before I commenced the autobiography I finished the history of the South African Passive Resistance. The original is in Gujarati. Its translation is now being published in instalments by Ganesan. I am afraid it will be some time before the whole history is available in English.

He finishes:

> *Do see Mr. Sastri, India's first Agent for South Africa. He is an extremely fine man. As you know he is Gokhale's successor. He knows all about you and is himself eager to see you.*

V. S. Srinivastri Sastri was interviewed by Schlesin at Gandhi's request and she sent him what Gandhi described as a "fascinating description of her interview with you". Sastri had succeeded Gokhale as the leader of the Servants of India Society and intended to stay in South Africa for only a year. He was a political moderate who often opposed Gandhi's radicalism.

Schlesin also didn't see eye-to-eye in all things and she wrote protesting about his change in dress. Gandhi responded:

> *... you have unconsciously altered the sense of my letter by mere atrocious reading. For, I did not suggest as you make me suggest that I could identify myself with the poor by merely wearing one garment. But I do say that even that little thing is something. To understand the logic of such a step is probably expecting too much of you now. For, there was a time when you appreciated my change of dress I adopted in Durban for almost identical considerations.*[31]

However they do agree that women should have the same educational opportunities as men and he assures her that women at the ashram have the utmost freedom.

Speaking at a meeting of women in November in Colombo he cited his critical friend as a good example of womanhood:

"... her defiant purity and innate fearlessness commanded in South Africa the adoration of thousands including among them fierce Pathans, robbers and questionable characters." [32]

Schlesin had been sending news of other former colleagues and friends and Gandhi ended the year with these words to Devi West: "Miss Schlesin has been of late writing to me regularly, and of course she is mad and as good as ever." [33]

In mid-1928 she resorted to criticism again; this time it was inaccuracies in the description of herself in Gandhi's autobiography where she was described as principal of a girls' school. She pointed out that she is a teacher in a high school – "to ask you *on no account* to publish the allusions to myself in your wretched autobiography in book-form until I send you a revised copy ..." Kallenbach then wrote to Gandhi saying: "Speaking about your autobiography, I do hope that Miss Schlesin is not hurting you with her eccentric criticism on a few sentences about her." Gandhi corrected his error in *Young India*. Shortly after in a letter to Manilal and Sushila Gandhi he wrote: "I follow what you say about Miss Schlesin. But, then, isn't she half crazy ? She has written a sort of wild letter even to me."

In February 1930 he seems to be actually expecting Schlesin to visit his ashram where Manilal, Sushila and their daughter Sita are visiting:

> *I do wish you will come in time to correct the many inaccuracies you have discovered in the volumes. It is highly likely that when your long leave is on I may be in one of the king's hotels* [prison]. *Even so, you will see my spirit incarnate in the ashram. It certainly brings into prominence all my shortcomings and some of my good points.*[34]

At the beginning of 1930 the Indian Declaration of Independence was proclaimed. On 12 March Gandhi set out from Sabarmati to march to Dandi using the salt tax as the focus of what was perhaps the greatest of his *satyagraha* campaigns. Before the end of the year 100,000 men and women had been imprisoned by the Raj.

In South Africa, Schlesin had taken up further study at this period and between 1929 and 1931 she took a Diploma in Afrikaans from the University of Witwatersrand. In 1931 she had once more raised the issue of his dress and Gandhi – writing with his left hand due to strain on his right from excessive writing – assured her: "There is nothing spectacular in the loin-cloth ... Do you know that millions in India do not wear anything more than a loin-cloth ? But I forgot you are a superior woman. You cannot judge people by the ordinary standard." He also wrote: "Well, I can't go to S. Africa since I am not even going to London." But about a week later he did decide to go to London for the Second Round Table Conference which was to be his last visit there.

The early 1930s saw some disagreements between Manilal and his father. Manilal was thinking of leaving Phoenix and moving the press to Durban, a move that Gandhi did not approve of. He was also thinking of a change of direction in that it seems he wanted to go to the USA and train in nature-cure, something that Schlesin may have suggested, but his father did not think it realistic. A further conflict came in 1934 over an article in *Indian Opinion* (edited by Manilal) in which he criticised Thambi Naidoo, the veteran *satyagrahi* who was now deceased. Gandhi supported Schlesin's position in defence of Thambi. An attack on the current Indian Agent by Manilal was also disliked by Schlesin and Gandhi upheld her position again.

VI

'Schlesie'

While Schlesin continued to follow Gandhi's career and the developments in India throughout her life, the main focus of her life was now in teaching. As one can imagine her dedication was total. Her favourite subject was Latin and we are told that she read it for enjoyment as well as teaching it. Homer was also a favourite with her (although I do not know if she could read it in the original Greek), but she loathed Geography as being too mundane. Latin students preparing for the certificate examinations were expected to attend classes in Latin on Saturday mornings. This certainly brought results as there were only two matric failures in 22 years. Elsje Coleman (née Stigant) a former pupil recalls: "The class of 1941 was Miss Schlesin's 21st matric class and she had her second failure. The student had come from another school in August and failed all six subjects. Schlesie remarked acerbically that at least he had made a good job of it." [35]

To her pupils she was an outstanding teacher but decidedly eccentric. As a result rumours spread about her and her family, many of which were pure invention. What was true was that she lived alone in a house called 'The Hermitage' in Sievewright Street from which she could walk to school. They knew she was a strict vegetarian – at one time eating only raw fruit and vegetables - and did not drink alcohol. Moira Soffe Bold was a pupil of Schlesin's in the few years up to 1940 when her teacher was nearing the end of her teaching career and she described her appearance as small, thin, bent, with grizzled dark greying curly hair cut short; she wore flat sandals, had false teeth which tended to click, and wore glasses. She was untidy with, for example, a petticoat showing in spite of long skirts. Her handwriting was poor and her initials on reports were an irregular 'Z ' turned through 90 degrees. It was the custom at that time for pupils to give presents to teachers at Christmas but Schlesin always promptly returned them. Moira Soffe was given a severe lecture by 'Schlesie' (as the pupils called her) one day for turning up at school with her hair elaborately curled – the reason being that she was to play Becky Sharp in *Vanity Fair* in the school that evening. Moira Soffe was however grateful to her for recommending that she study medicine, advice that she took and never regretted. [36]

In 1937 she acquired donations of more than 1000 books for the school library which she classified with the help of pupils after studying the system of classification used in the municipal library. She was House Mistress of one of the 'Houses', Diaz, for many years.

Sometimes Schlesie would invite pupils to her home, for extra tuition, or perhaps because they were prefects. Once they had gone through the padlocked gate of The Hermitage and into the house they might see busts of Ovid and Virgil as well as a photograph of Gandhi. They might observe less elevated sights, though, such as the kitchen sink full of crockery which their teacher would wash once she had dirted all her dishes; or an unmade bed of which she had four which she would use in rotation as she hated making beds. Elsje Coleman relates: "She was always ready to learn, so she took a course in home nursing. In the theory section she attained 100%. For the practical, she had to make a bed and got 0."

Former pupil Stella Israelsohn (née Klein) recalls: "Teaching was her life, and she understood the foibles of her students. An errant pupil who had not done her homework chose to copy ten sentences of translation into Latin from ten students at random, so that it would appear to be her own work. Her effort was returned with the initials of each source neatly printed beside the corresponding sentence !" [37]

It is not surprising that Schlesin was never promoted (although it is possible that she was not interested either) because it seems she was not the easiest of colleagues and did not tolerate any interference in her work. Traces of a clash can be found in the Principal's logbook in 1940:
"1.3.40. Miss Schlesin took upon herself to write to the local inspector, calling in question the instructions re 'Supplementary Examination' at which he had ordered her to do two hours' invigilation. The inspector's reply is filed and reads: 'I am directed to inform you that the proper conduct of the examination to which you refer rests with the Principal who is the Commissioner, and you are to carry out his instructions.'
6.3.40 The headmaster warned Miss Schlesin to mind her own business."

Schlesin put great store on education and hard work. Perhaps she saw this as particularly important for women as they could achieve economic independence through this route. One of her friends was Dr. Susie Blake who practised in Delareyville, a small Western Transvaal village. Susie Blake was one of the first women to qualify in medicine at Witwatersrand, beginning her studies at the age of 39, it being an economic struggle for her. For this Schlesin admired her and placed her photograph on a top shelf next to Gandhi. However when Blake married, relatively late in life, Schlesin demoted her picture to a lower shelf. A few years later Blake adopted two children and the picture was then placed on an even lower shelf.[38]

Susie Blake's niece, Ruth Keech, who related the story also recalled meeting Schlesin in 1940 when she was about ten years old. On the way with her mother to visit Blake they passed through Krugersdorp in the evening and were met by Schlesin at the station. Her mother said: "She thinks you look intelligent; she sets a lot of store by intelligence."

Another woman who as a child knew Schlesin was Sita Gandhi-Dhupelia, granddaughter of Mohandas and eldest daughter of Manilal Gandhi. Schlesin was a godmother to her and used to come to Phoenix in the school holidays. Schlesin's strong opinions once more featured because she disagreed with Gandhi over the name Sita. Sita of the *Ramayana* suffered a great deal throughout her life and Schlesin felt the girl should not be burdened with such a name. Sita's maternal grandfather had given her another name, Dhairyabala, which means 'maid of courage' and that is the one that Schlesin always called her by.[39]

Schlesin retired from teaching at the age of 55 in June 1943. However, it appears that she may then have joined the war effort in an administrative capacity, probably in the Defence Headquarters in Pretoria. It appears she prepared herself for this by doing some studies in Accountancy at Witwatersrand University during the previous year. She also went to college to brush up her shorthand but the readers were not fast enough for her. Many of Gandhi's former colleagues who were of Jewish origin departed from Gandhi's pacifist position during the Nazi period and so it may have been with Schlesin. Although it seems improbable, it is reported that she supported during the war the United Party Government led by her old antagonist Jan Christian Smuts. This seems possible when one remembers that the Government was anti-Nazi, and moreover Smuts was pro-Jewish and Zionist and advocated free entry of Jews into South Africa. He was not however sympathetic to black African aspirations.

VII

Nonviolence, the Nazis and the Jews

Surprisingly for someone so committed to nonviolence Gandhi actually participated – in a noncombatant capacity – in three wars. The first was the Anglo-Boer War when he recruited more than a thousand Indians to form an ambulance corps which was deployed eventually in the field of battle. It consisted of Muslims and Hindus, indentured labourers and professional people who acquitted themselves well. In 1906 during the so-called Bambatha Rebellion a small corps of 20 Indians treated Zulus whom the Europeans would not help. Gandhi held the rank of sergeant-major on this occasion. The third occasion was at the start of the Great War when Gandhi had left South Africa for the last time and was making his way to India via London. About 80 Indian students were recruited and trained and although Gandhi himself fell ill, the corps was asked to help nurse wounded soldiers who has been brought back to Britain from the Front.

Gandhi was criticised by Henry Polak for involving himself in war even if in a non-combatant capacity. In fact Gandhi agreed that his participation was an involvement in war but his main argument for it seemed to be that a community which accepted the advantages of living in a protective environment, and which could potentially be accepted as equal under the law, had a duty to defend that state, especially since most Indians had no objection to fighting in principle. However when Gandhi actually started recruiting for the British Army in India in 1918 he had gone a step too far for most of his supporters. Charlie Andrews and Henry Polak were strong in their criticism of his actions, which were also largely unsuccessful as even the ordinary Indian whom he hoped to persuade to join the Army could see the contradiction in the great advocate of nonviolence asking people to join the armed forces. Although he later defended his actions one must regard this episode as an aberration, as a failure of good judgement, and it is difficult not to think that the overriding motive in this period, and to some extent in the earlier events, was that he believed that if the Indians were seen by the British to be supporting them in a time of difficulty they would look more favourably on their post-war appeals for political autonomy. That Gandhi fell seriously ill at this time has sometimes been interpreted, not unreasonably, as a result of an inner conflict arising from his own belief in nonviolence accompanied by his advocacy to others of the military way.

On the ending of the War, the Raj failed to appreciate what Gandhi had tried to do and enacted the repressive Rowlatt Act which was then followed by the Amritsar Massacre. Gandhi's faith in the British Empire as a force for good, an opinion that had wavered for years, finally ended. Nonviolent opposition to the Raj came to the fore and soon he was to find himself in prison. He was to disappoint Western pacifists again in the coming years when he accepted the demand of Congress to take control of India's own forces. His rather convoluted position of, on the one hand, hoping for an Indian state that would dispense with armed forces, and on the other, saying publicly that India needed to take its own decision on this which might mean having armed forces, led to criticism by the prominent Dutch pacifist Bart de Ligt. At the same time, for example in Paris, Geneva and Laussane on his way back from the Round Table Conference in London, he was recommending nonviolent defence to the European countries. Certainly for the remainder of his life the emphasis was on nonviolence as a method for liberating India and for defence of any country against invaders .

During the 1930s Gandhi's faith in the power of nonviolence grew and he advocated non-cooperation to the Ethiopians in their resistance to Fascist Italy in 1935, to the Czechoslovaks under threat from Nazi Germany in 1938, even to the major military powers of France and Britain, and to his own country when it was threatened with invasion by the forces of Japan in 1940. He did not however work out a detailed plan of resistance even in the case of India, although he did not advocate inclusion of a scorched-earth policy His sometimes contradictory statements on armed defence can, I think, be explained by the two levels at which he operated. He was opposed to armed violence even in a good cause and strove to spread and demonstrate the effectiveness of nonviolence but on the other hand he sometimes felt compelled to make statements in situations where it was clear that nonviolence was not going to be used. Here he thought it better that others act with courage in a good cause even if it involved violence. The last occasion on which he offered such an opinion was after the invasion of Kashmir when he reluctantly gave his support to the new Government of India in its military defence of Kashmir. Periodically since then, successive Indian Governments and ordinary Indians have been using this statement of reluctant support to justify all kinds of armed actions and preparations for war. It might have been better for him to have refrained from any statement where he was powerless to influence the situation.

Perhaps his most controversial stance was with regard to the Jews, particularly those of Germany. In the 26 November 1938 issue of *Harijan* he, "with hesitation", offered his views:

> *My sympathies are all with the Jews. I have known them intimately in South Africa. Some of them became life-long companions. Through these friends I came to learn much of their age-long persecution. They have been the untouchables of Christianity.*[40]

After expressing his view that a separate state of Palestine for the Jews is not justified because it would mean displacing the Arabs he continued:

> *But the German persecution of the Jews seems to have no parallel in history. The tyrants of old never went so mad as Hitler seems to have gone. And he is doing it with religious zeal. For, he is propounding a new religion of exclusive and militant nationalism in the name of which any inhumanity becomes an act of humanity to be rewarded here and hereafter [....] If there ever could be a justifiable war in the name of and for humanity, a war against Germany, to prevent the wanton persecution of a whole race, would be completely justified. But I do not believe in any war. A discussion of the pros and cons of such a war is, therefore, outside my horizon or province.*
>
> *[....] Can the Jews resist this organised and shameless persecution ? Is there a way to preserve their self-respect, and not to feel helpless, neglected and forlorn ? I submit there is. No person who has faith in a living God need feel helpless or forlorn. Jehovah of the Jews is a God more personal than the God of the Christians, the Musalmans or the Hindus, though as a matter of fact, in essence, He is common to all and one without a second and beyond description. But as the Jews attribute personality to God and believe that He rules every action of theirs, they ought not to feel helpless. If I were a Jew and were born in Germany and earned my livelihood there, I would claim Germany as my home even as the tallest gentile German might, and challenge him to shoot me or cast me in the dungeon; I would refuse to be expelled or to submit to discriminating treatment. And for doing this I should not wait for the fellow Jews to join me in civil resistance, but would have confidence that in the end the rest were bound to follow my example. If one Jew or all the Jews were to accept the prescription here offered, he or they cannot be worse off than now. And*

suffering voluntarily undergone will bring them an inner strength and joy which no number of resolutions of sympathy passed in the world outside Germany can. Indeed, even if Britain, France and America were to declare hostilities against Germany, they can bring no inner joy, no inner strength. The calculated violence of Hitler may even result in a general massacre of the Jews by way of his first answer to the declaration of such hostilities. But if the Jewish mind could be prepared for voluntary suffering, even the massacre I have imagined could be turned into a day of thanksgiving and joy that Jehovah had wrought deliverance of the race even at the hands of the tyrant.

[...] the Jews of Germany can offer Satyagraha under infinitely better auspices than the Indians of South Africa. The Jews are a compact, homogeneous community in Germany. They are far more gifted than the Indians of South Africa. And they have organised world opinion behind them. I am convinced that, if someone with courage and vision can arise among them to lead them in non-violent action, the winter of their despair can in the twinkling of an eye be turned into the summer of hope. And what has today become a degrading man-hunt can be turned into a calm and determined stand offered by unarmed men and women possessing the strength of suffering given to them by Jehovah. It will be then a truly religious resistance offered against the godless fury of dehumanised man. The German Jews will score a lasting victory over the German gentiles in the sense that they will have converted the latter to an appreciation of human dignity. They will have rendered service to fellow-Germans and proved their title to be the real Germans as against those who are today dragging, however unknowingly, the German name into the mire.

In the same article however Gandhi had dealt with the Palestinian issue and apparently applied double standards when he justified – "according to the accepted standards of right and wrong" – Palestinian defence of their territory. It may have been some sort of unconscious compliment to the Jews in expecting them to rise to a higher moral level than the Palestinians but it was not appreciated.

But, leaving aside the Palestinian issue, his recommendation of nonviolence to the German Jews was considered totally unrealistic by many, including Martin Buber and Judah L. Magnes who wrote a response. While they were correct in stating that the position of the Jews in Germany was much worse than that of the Indians of South Africa, what did the critics of Gandhi expect the German Jews to do ? They were certainly in no position to offer violent resistance themselves, and the Allies' war against Nazi Germany did not save the Jews either.

But Britain, the USA and some other countries could certainly be criticised for not having an open door policy towards continental Jews when the persecution began. Other than fleeing, nonviolent resistance was the only option, except lying low and hoping that one would be one of the lucky ones. This latter was never Gandhi's way and in this case it proved ineffective also in most instances.

Gandhi was probably unrealistic if he expected Hitler and the Nazis to be converted by nonviolent suffering to a humane outlook but, on the other hand, nonviolent resistance – sometimes of a pragmatic kind, sometimes a result of principled belief – was used in many situations during the Second World War, particularly in the countries occupied by German forces. Many sectors of the Norwegian population organised nonviolent resistance to defend their way of life with some significant success. Many people in other occupied countries organised to save their Jewish compatriots and many more individuals did what they could at great risk to themselves to save Jews or other opponents of the Nazis. Many thousands of Jews were saved; tens of thousands of Hungarian Jews by the Swede Raoul Wallenberg alone. [41]

Regarding Zionism, who can say that Gandhi was completely wrong in opposing the settlement of Palestine by the Jews when more than half a century after its creation it is one of the principal sources of conflict in the world ?

What position Schlesin held on these issues is not known but if it is true that she joined the South African Defence Department then she would have supported armed resistance to the Nazis.

VIII

Last Years

In January 1945 correspondence resumed between the two old friends:

> *I do not think there is any chance of my coming to S. Africa or going to America. But whether I do or not, of course I expect you one day to drop in here and pass the rest of your days in India. Of course it may be that the climate here does not suit you as it did neither Kallenbach nor Hannah [that is Hannah Lazar, Kallenbach's niece].*[42]

Schlesin was actually expecting to meet her old colleague at the Peace Conference in San Francisco which established the United Nations Organisation and go – at last – with him back to India. "If you are short of secretaries to accompany you to the Peace Conference, call here on your way and I shall come along." But in a letter of 13 May Gandhi wrote: "So you see, San Francisco was managed without you and me."

On hearing of Kallenbach's death in March, Gandhi wrote to Schlesin saying that "a truly good man has left us". Although Kallenbach had not followed his friend to India either, he had visited Sevagram Ashram in 1937, and again in 1939 but he became seriously ill with malaria on the latter occasion. Over the years Kallenbach had become a strong supporter of Jewish settlement of Palestine although he believed it should be with the support of the Palestinian Arabs.[43]

In 1946 Sonja's mother Helena, whom she had helped to support financially since the death of her husband in 1921, died. Dorothy Schlesin, whose husband was a first cousin, knew Sonja's sister Rose but only met Sonja on one occasion, that is shortly before Helena Schlesin died when they met in the mother's flat. Sonja's behaviour was characteristically out of the ordinary. Apparently she did not speak to anyone except that she came up to Dorothy Schlesin and said: "You are a very nice person and I like you".[44]

That same year Schlesin was discussing, through correspondence, economics with Gandhi who apparently agreed with her – "A highly industrial system under capitalism and full employment are incompatible".

In October Schlesin wrote:

> *Far from losing your desire to live until you are 125, increasing knowledge of the world's lovelessness and consequent misery should cause you rather to determine to live longer still ... You said in a letter to me some time ago that everyone ought to wish to attain the age of 125, you can't go back on that.*[45]

Later she wrote:

> *The Aga Khan ... is reported as saying ... that the cloud that hangs over India is your old age. Is it possible that he has not heard of your decision to live until you are 125 or does he not understand ? In any case your decision has now lifted that cloud, for you are once again in the springtime of life, a more wonderful springtime because enriched by the experience of the years – why, your very handwriting seems to have taken on new vigour. You speak of writing the experience of those 125 years. I hope I shall be privileged to share in the sub-editing of at least a part of that volume.*[46]

Schlesin was 59 when Gandhi was gunned down on 30 January 1948. In 1953 at age 65 she enrolled at the University of Natal – to study law. Michael Imber (later Attorney-General for Natal) was a student in her class and recalled how the other students considered it odd for someone of her age to be in their class. She kept very much to herself and although they knew she was *the* Schlesin in the 1909 case they did not know that her sponsor was *the* Gandhi.[47] However she was not able to complete her degree as she withdrew on 14 March 1955, presumably because of ill health for she died on 6 January 1956 in Johannesburg General Hospital having been looked after in her last months by her sister Rose.

Her body was cremated and Rose arranged for a plaque to be placed on the Wall of Remembrance of Braamfontein Cemetery, Johannesburg. It reads:

IN MEMORY
OF
MY SISTER
SONJA SCHLESIN

DIED 6 JANUARY 1956
HER LIFE WAS DEDICATED
TO THE SERVICE OF OTHERS

IX

Schlesin the Woman

Sonja Schlesin worked with Gandhi during one of the most active periods of his life, his late 30s and early 40s at a time when he was rapidly developing. She contributed greatly, along with a few other Europeans, to his public campaigns. His departure for India in 1914 however marked a break. The Polaks did spend some time in India supporting him but eventually settled in Britain; Kallenbach did not visit India until much later and did not settle there either; Schlesin did not make even one visit to Gandhi's homeland. Most of the other European colleagues did not visit India either. This seems to have been a disappointment to Gandhi. Schlesin's remaining in South Africa may have been no more than an attachment to her family, combined with her determination to finish her academic studies, and then, finding satisfaction in teaching, she may have seen no reason to become a follower of the now leader of the Indian independence movement.

However they did both feel a bond that lasted for the rest of their lives. Gandhi pleaded with Schlesin many times to come to India to help in his public work, especially in developing his educational programme. And Schlesin kept a photograph of her friend in her house and continued to correspond with him, if not very frequently, throughout his life.

A continuous strand that ran through Schlesin's life was what we would now call feminism. She seemed to possess greater confidence than tact and expressed herself rather bluntly, which sometimes led to uneasy relationships, as with Kallenbach and Ritch, and later with at least one headteacher of Krugersdorp High. At the earliest possible age she applied for articleship in law and was the first woman in South Africa to do so, although she did not achieve the historic breakthrough. We know she was a strong supporter of the aims of the women's suffrage movement.

What is equally interesting is Gandhi's position here. The British suffragettes, in the pre-violent phase, were one of the influences on the development of *satyagraha*. And of course Gandhi was intended to be Schlesin's educator in the legal profession, being her sponsor, so he was a feminist of some sort at this fairly early stage in his life. Later in India he took up the cause of women by his opposition to *purdah*, to child marriage, to the custom forbidding remarriage of widows, and he promoted equality in education. In his own life, particularly in South Africa, he carried out household tasks usually done by women, he delivered his last child after reading a book on midwifery, and he took every opportunity to nurse those who were ill. During the independence campaigns women, especially from the time of the Salt March, played a major role and thousands went to prison, as indeed had smaller numbers in the later phase of *satyagraha* in South Africa. His colleagues in India included many women and some, like Sarojini Naidu, Rajkumari Amrit Kaur and Sushila Nayar, became government ministers after independence.

Even more remarkable is that as early as 1895 the Natal Indian Congress admitted to membership two women, Raboobe and Lutchminia, no doubt with the encouragement of Gandhi.[48] Such 'feminism' was not common, as he wrote in *Indian Opinion* in 1909: "Those who pose as reformers as also other well-to-do Indians, whether Hindu or Muslim, Parsi or Christian, either treat their women as playthings or use them as they fancy for self-indulgence ..." [49] From a different angle, if it had not been for a white woman Gandhi might never have become known to history, for on disembarking from ship in Durban in 1897 he was attacked by a mob of whites. The quick thinking of Jane Alexander, wife of the Police Superintendent, who put up her parasol over him, saved him from severe injury and possible death.

Their abhorrence of another form of discrimination – racism – must also have drawn Gandhi and Schlesin to each other. Schlesin was aware of what Gandhi had been doing before she became his secretary and she was impressed. Gandhi had hardly been aware of discrimination on racial grounds until he encountered it in South Africa, while Schlesin must have been aware of it through her parents' experience of it in eastern Europe. Their work together was on behalf only of the Asian community of South Africa, but Gandhi's pioneering human rights campaigns were an influence on the African National Congress in the years to come, and Manilal settled in South Africa and became involved in the general anti-racist movement. I am not aware of any public activity by Schlesin on behalf of the races discriminated against in the four decades after Gandhi's departure but we have some evidence of her outlook from her will that was drawn up in 1939. In this will she bequeathed her teacher's pension to her mother who had been a widow since 1921, and the rest of her estate was bequeathed to her sister Rose. However if both died before her then her estate was to be used to establish a scholarship at the University of Witwatersrand. All her money was to be handed to Professor Jan Hendrik Hofmeyr, Chancellor of the University "for the establishment of a Scholarship, to be known as the Rose and Robert Schlesin Memorial Scholarship and to be open to all students irrespective of race, colour or creed, but to be awarded on qualities of character as well as of intellect". The last point is also notable. In the event Rose survived her and inherited her modest estate. Her relative by marriage, Dorothy Schlesin, also believed she had contacts with Fort Hare, the pioneering college for black students.

The second, and longest, phase of Schlesin's life began with Gandhi's departure from South Africa. She concentrated on her university studies at which, not surprisingly with her will-power, she excelled. She then settled in the modest Transvaal town of Krugersdorp where her whole teaching career was spent, her subject – which she loved – being Latin. She not only knew her subject but she was an effective teacher who won the respect of her pupils. We do not know of any friendships with colleagues and she appears to have become more solitary as she aged. Unlike Gandhi she valued education and learning for its own sake, although she no doubt saw it as of particular value to those who started from disadvantage. While Gandhi valued religious and ethical writings, his interest was in applying these ideas and principles in his life and to society in an original way. In contrast it is difficult to see that there would have been any practical value in Schlesin taking up the study of law when over 60 years of age so perhaps it was the intellectual challenge that was the motive. Schlesin's more normal life post-1914 contrasts with Gandhi's immensely active life as a major world figure with huge demands on his time and energy. It is astonishing that he could still keep up contacts with so many people including Schlesin and other former South African colleagues.

There is one aspect of life which both Gandhi and Schlesin found difficult to come to terms with – and that is sexual relations. Schlesin never seems to have had a close personal relationship and she was embarrassed in the presence of those with an obvious relationship of that sort. While Gandhi was married at 13 years of age and had children, it was not his choice. Although at one stage he encouraged his friends to get married, after he adopted celibacy in his 30s he tried to persuade colleagues and friends to renounce sexual relationships, even advocating marriages that were entirely celibate. We do not know the reason for Schlesin's difficulty but, as described earlier, we have a good idea of its origin in Gandhi's life. Gandhi however turned this negative characteristic into a virtue. Abstention enabled him, he believed, to carry out the tasks which he had set himself by giving him the necessary energy, an idea that stems from a traditional Hindu belief. But Gandhi's celibacy did not prevent him from having loving relationships with women, or indeed men; having ruled out sexual relationships, it made those asexual ones easy and relaxed. Unlike some religious celibates he did not avoid those of the opposite gender but had easy natural relationships with them. Nevertheless his universalising of the virtues of celibacy was not necessarily good advice.

Regarding religion, we have little detailed evidence but Schlesin did develop a particular interest in Christianity and seems to have joined a Methodist Church at some time during her teaching career. It is very likely however that, like Gandhi, her beliefs were inclusive of different religious traditions.

Gandhi's most important legacy – the application of the principle of nonviolence to politics – is still controversial and not widely accepted. But the use of nonviolent direct action as a supplement to traditional democratic action is now familiar, as is the overthrow of authoritarian regimes (eg in Europe from the Polish Solidarity movement onwards), but belief in the armed state and the defence of one's interests through military force is still the norm. Yet even where there is a good cause, such as defence against invasion as in the Falkland Islands or Kuwait, or defence of human rights as in Kosovo, Afghanistan or Iraq, the cost in terms of lives lost (predominantly civilian), life-long disablement, environmental damage, among others, is immense. Another negative effect of the military way is the diversion of economic resources which could reduce the grinding poverty and ill-health of millions. The reduction of poverty itself would increase security. We do not know for certain if Schlesin followed Gandhi in his evolving nonviolence – although we know she was a strict vegetarian. If it is true that she joined the Defence Department during WWII then it is likely that she followed many of her fellow Jews in believing that Nazism had to be resisted if necessary by counter-violence. Einstein, who was in general a pacifist, made an exception of Nazism. Of course this was by no means confined to Jews – Bertrand Russell abandoned pacifism in the face of Nazism, as did thousands of others. Most people would still agree that that was the right decision. But with some 50 million deaths resulting from that conflict and the resulting inauguration of the nuclear era with its still real threat of mass extermination, the cost was – and is – extremely high.

We need as a society to lose faith in the effectiveness of the military path and substitute for it the path of nonviolence. This was Gandhi's hope. This has nothing to do with a passive approach to social and political issues but is, as we can see in Gandhi's life, an extremely active force. This is not a new idea, as Gandhi said – "it is as old as the hills", and its effectiveness is being increasingly demonstrated by ordinary people around the world.

The life patterns of the two figures we have followed were quite different. Schlesin exhibited early academic ability and while still in her teenage years was confident of her abilties and judgement. At the same age Gandhi was of modest academic attainment, shy and uncertain. He was a slow developer, but unlike most people he never ceased developing and evolving, never stopped questioning the world around him and was driven by an exceptional force of will to try to change himself and change society for the better. Gandhi made his mark on history, and still does; Schlesin is forgotten. Perhaps it is the difference between a talented individual and what we call genius, the latter being able to see the world in a fresh way and express it in some form that others recognise as a new insight. One must not forget however that Schlesin had, a century ago, the disadvantage of her gender.

Nevertheless Schlesin possessed many admirable qualities. Respect for the truth as one sees it, and courageously defending it, was a quality she shared with her friend – she was a *satyagrahi* in the broad sense. Both cared little for personal comforts or possessions. Interestingly her acqaintances all describe her appearance and dress, which was unchanging and an expression of her personality. She took objection to Gandhi's change to an Indian peasant form of dress yet they both became identified by their 'uniform'. She paid attention to what she regarded as important and was careless of other matters no matter what other people thought, hence her 'eccentricity'. Gandhi likewise was considered odd in some of his habits.

Both had a strong sense of justice and injustice, both were highly disciplined individuals. But perhaps she lacked in later life the ability to express the natural human warmth which Gandhi exuded. She was undoubtedly empathetic but did not find it easy to express her feelings.

Gandhi's influence extended not just throughout a large country but round the world and into the future; the influence of Sonja Schlesin, like that of most of us, was largely confined to those with whom she came in direct contact. Both Schlesin and Gandhi undoubtedly lived lives of service and achieved a degree of fullfilment in doing so.

Notes

The Collected Works of Mahatma Gandhi (CWMG) references are from the CD produced for the Publications Division, Ministry of Information and Broadcasting, Government of India, 1999.

1. In 1999 the then President of the Natal Law Society announced: "The Society apologises unconditionally, albeit posthumously, to the late Mahatma Gandhi for having attempted to restrict his rights to practice in Natal, as well as to all other aspirant lawyers whose access was restricted in any way over the years on the basis of racial grounds."
2. *Satyagraha in South Africa* Revised edition 1950 pp 164-5.
3. Interview to *The Jewish Chronicle* 1931. Cited in Hunt *Gandhi and the Nonconformists.*
4. Phoenix Settlement had been owned by Thomas Watkins whose first crop of sugar cane was destroyed by fire. He replanted in the ashes of the burned crop so Watkins called his farm Phoenix. Gandhi wrote in a letter to Maganlal Gandhi on 24 November 1909: " 'Phoenix' is a very good word which has come to us without any effort on our part.... Its significance, as the legend goes, is that the bird phoenix comes back to life again and again from its own ashes, ie it never dies. The name Phoenix, for the present, serves the purpose quite well, for we believe the aims of Phoenix will not vanish even when we are turned to dust."
5. The Empire Theatre was accidentally destroyed by fire that night.
6. CWMG Vol. 8 : 47
7. In 1913 the leading Jewish synagogue was built on this vacant site.
8. CWMG Vol. 8 : 79
9. CWMG Vol. 8 : 114
10. *The Transvaal Leader* 26/4/1909 – summary of the court decision.
11. *Indian Opinion* 10/5/1913. CWMG Vol 13 : 82.
12. *The Story of My Experiments with Truth* Navajivan Ch XII.
13. Gokhale quoted in Tendulkar *Mahatma* 1;112.
14. Eric Itzkin *Gandhi's Johannesburg: Birthplace of Satyagraha* pp10-11.
15. A PS by Schlesin on a letter from Ritch to Gandhi 15/4/1911 (from notes by James Hunt).
16. *Indian Opinion* 31/8/1912. CWMG Vol 12 : 204

17. Quoted in *Satyagraha in South Africa* Ch XXIII.

18. Prabhudas Gandhi *Jivanu Parodh* (*The Dawn of Life*) Navajivan 1948. Extract from English version edited by James Hunt.

19. CWMG Vol. 15 : 116

20. CWMG Vol. 15 : 362 Talk with teachers of the National School, Ahmedabad (founded by MKG) 23/6/1917.

21. CWMG Vol. 15: 410

22. One of his more dubious decisions, surely. Although he gave as the reason the requirement to perform one's duty as a subject of the Empire, another motive was that he hoped the British Government would respond to Indian aspirations after the War. A similar belief led Jews in Germany to join the army in large numbers during the wars of liberation against Napoleon and again a century later during the First World War.

23. CWMG Vol. 17 : 72

24. CWMG Vol. 17 : 285

25. CWMG Vol. 18 : 66

26. Printed version CWMG Vol. 96 : 279

27. CWMG Vol. 24 : 177

28. CWMG Vol. 28 : 292

29. Communication through Ivan Elion, Jewish Genealogical Society Johannesburg.

30. CWMG Vol. 38 : 425

31. CWMG Vol. 39 : 392

32. CWMG Vol. 40 : 279

33. CWMG Vol. 41 : 53

34. CWMG Vol. 48 : 291

35. From a still to be published history of Krugersdorp High School by Sharon Farrell.

36. Communication (28/9/97) from Dr Moira Soffe Bold who was a pupil of Schlesin in the late 1930s and 1940.

37. Sharon Farrell.

38. Communication (25/10/97) from Ruth Keech, Cape Town.

39. Communication (20/10/97) from Sita Gandhi-Dhupelia, Durban.

40. *Nonviolence in Peace and War* Vol.1 Navajivan pp170-174.

41. Roger S. Powers, '"But What About Hitler ?": Nonviolent Resistance Against Nazism' *Fellowship* May/June 1995.

42. CWMG Vol. 86 : 498

43. Today there is a Kallenbach Drive in the North East Johannesburg suburb of Linksfield, and a Hannebahn Street named after his niece Hannah Lazar.

44. Communication (17/3/97) from Dorothy Schlesin, Johannesburg.

45. Footnote to letter in CWMG Vol. 97 : 182.

46. Pyarelal *The Last Phase Vol. 1, Book 1* Navajivan 1965 p102.

47. Communication from Michael Imber SC 14/8/2000.

48. Burnett Britton *Gandhi Arrives in South Africa* p 290.

49. Burnett Britton Ch. 8, note 10.

Schlesin with Gandhi and Kallenbach

Gandhi being arrested 1913. Kallenbach and Schlesin are on either side of him.

Staff of Krugersdorp High School 1936. Schlesin is in middle row, 3rd from right.

Krugersdorp High School in 1914.
The building is now the regional school office and no longer has the bell-tower.

Profiles

Alexander, Sarah Jane (b.1849) Wife of Richard C. Alexander, the Durban Superintendent of Police from 1876 to 1906. She rescued Gandhi when attacked after leaving the *SS Courland* on 13 January 1897. A pamphlet by Gandhi summarising the position of Indians in South Africa had been published while he was back in India and a report of this exaggerating Gandhi's criticism had reached South Africa thus leading to a mob of over 3000 gathering to meet the ship at Durban. The ship was quarantined for 24 days before the Indians were allowed to land and Gandhi was persuaded to disembark separately from other passengers with a solicitor, Frederick Laughton, but the crowd spotted him. After the rescue he was taken to the police station and then smuggled (to avert an attack on the police station) to Parsi Rustomji's house. The Alexanders were given gifts of gold watches by the Indian community in appreciation. At a farewell meeting in 1914 Gandhi recalled the kindness and resourcefulness of Mrs Alexander.

Ally, Haji Ojer (b.1853) He was born in Mauritius and emigrated to the Cape in 1884 where he set up a soda water business. He married a Cape Malay and became involved in Coloured politics from 1885. In 1892 he was elected Chairman of the Coloured People's Organisation which raised 10,000 signatures against the move to deprive Coloureds of franchise rights. He was a voter prior to moving to the Transvaal. He became the first President of the Hamidia Islamic Society established in July 1906 in Johannesburg (it was named after Sultan Hamid of the Ottoman Empire). The Society, which was established for the social welfare of Muslims, played an important role in the 1906 meeting of all Indians. He travelled on delegation with Gandhi to London in 1906 but was ill with rheumatism while there and was treated by Gandhi's friend from his students days, Dr Josiah Oldfield. He returned to the Cape with his family in August 1907, being in poor health. By May 1909 most Transvaal Asians had given up resistance. In June Ally and Habib, who had returned to Transvaal, tried for a final negotiated settlement which failed and *satyagraha* was resorted to.

Ampthill, Lord (1869-1935) 2nd Baron. Arthur Russell, educated at Eton College and New College, Oxford. Governor of Madras 1899-

1906, Acting Viceroy 1904. Grand Master of the Grand Lodge of England. In November 1906 he was appointed Chairman of the South African British Indian Committee (Ritch was Secretary). During the 1909 visit to London of Gandhi, he advised quiet diplomacy rather than public statements. He was a conservative and imperialist and his concern was perhaps more to do with the smooth running of the Empire than with equal rights. Ampthill wrote an introduction to Doke's short biography of Gandhi. On 18 June 1913 he deplored the passage of the Immigration Bill. On 30 July he requested the Government to suspend operation of the Act until amended to the satisfaction of the Indians. In December 1913 a Commission of Enquiry was set up but it was boycotted by the Indians, which Ampthill regretted. When *satyagraha* was withdrawn after white railway workers struck, Ampthill was pleased.

Andrews, Rev. Charles Freer (1871-1940) He was brought up in the Catholic Apostolic Church of which his parents were ardent adherents. He won a Classical Scholarship to Pembroke College, Cambridge and became an Anglican priest at Southwark Cathedral in 1897. Here he came face to face with poverty in this part of London. In 1899 he became a Fellow of Pembroke College. Bishop Westcott of Durham aroused his interest in India and he took a post with the Cambridge Brotherhood at St Stephen's College, Delhi, in March 1904. Vice-Principal Susil Kumar Rudra and Andrews became close friends. In 1906 Andrews invited Rudra to stay for a few days at a school for sons and daughters of soldiers in Simla which was greatly resented by an English colleague. He put all his weight in favour of Rudra to succeed to the principalship of St Stephen's College and was successful. He first met Gokhale in December 1906 at the Calcutta Congress of the INC. In June 1912 Andrews met Rabindranath Tagore in Britain. Gokhale met him again in late 1913 when Gokhale was fund raising for the South African cause. Andrews offered £300 for South Africa but Gokhale only accepted £75. Gokhale then asked him to go to South Africa with Andrews' friend Rev. William Pearson and they arrived there early in January 1914. They were met by Gandhi, Polak, Kallenbach, and other Indians at Durban. They were surprised that Gandhi was out of prison. Andrews knelt and touched Gandhi's feet, an act that was criticised in the press the next day. Soon they were 'Mohan' and 'Charlie' to each other. When Andrews preached in Natal Cathedral, Gandhi and Pearson were refused entry. Andrews was at first opposed to Gandhi's boycott of a Commission of Enquiry because of its composition but he and Pearson were won over. The two went to Pretoria to meet Smuts and their mediation was important for the final outcome. Back in India Andrews went to Tagore's Shantiniketan in April 1914. He investigated the 1919 Amritsar massacre and reported to the Hunter Commission. During the next two decades he visited east and south Africa, Fiji, British Guiana, Canada and indeed everywhere that Indians had settled. In 1929-30 while touring the USA he opposed a Bill to admit Indians to the USA on an equal footing with Europeans on the grounds that they were Ayrans – he regarded this as racist. He advocated independence for India but did not always support Gandhi's methods and opposed bonfires of foreign cloth. When Gandhi visited Britain in 1931 Andrews arranged for him to meet many prominent figures. He took up many causes – opium traffic, relief to victims of famine, earthquakes, riots, and supported workers in factories and on estates. He wrote 25 books and many articles. His lifestyle was simple and he rarely had money because he gave it away as he believed a Christian should.

Besant, Annie (1847-1933) Feminist, socialist, theosophist. Annie Wood married clergyman, Frank Besant, at 20 and had a son and a daughter to him but the marriage was unhappy. After six years she left her husband, taking her daughter. She met the atheist Charles Bradlaugh and both of them were prosecuted for publishing a book on contraception and this led to Annie losing custody of both of her children. She was also one of the first women to study science at London University. In 1885 she joined the Fabian Society and became a lecturer for them. She led a strike of girls working at a match factory in 1888. The following year she met Madame Blavatsky and quickly became a leading figure in the Theosophical Society. As a student Gandhi was impressed by her speeches. In 1893 she visited India and she was soon to make it her home. She also involved herself in Indian politics and was President of the INC in 1917. Her political influence diminished after 1920 as Gandhi came to the fore.

Botha, Louis (1862-1919) Farmer, soldier and politician. Commander in the Transvaal during the Anglo-Boer War (1899-1902), during which he organised guerrilla warfare, and captured Winston Churchill. He became Premier of the Transvaal in 1907 and in 1910-19 was Prime Minister of the Union of South Africa. He opposed Paul Kruger's hostility to non-Boers (*uitlanders*). He supported the Allies in the First World War and defeated the Germans in SW Africa in 1915. He advocated leniency at the peace conference in Versailles.

Buber, Martin (1878-1965) Theologian/philosopher. He was born in Vienna to non-practising Jews and studied at the Universities of Leipzig, Zurich and Vienna. He married Paula Winkler, a Catholic writer who shared his intellectual interests. He introduced mystic Hasidism which had origininated in Eastern Europe to the Jews of the West. He edited *Der Jude* (The Jew) 1916-24 which advocated a binational state in Palestine. Professor at University of Frankfurt 1920-33, Professor at the Hebrew University, Jerusalem from 1938. A prolific writer on the philosophy and sociology of religion and on Hasidism. His best known work is *I and Thou*. He died in Jerusalem.

Cachalia, Ahmed Mohammed (d.1918) A Gujarati, he arrived in Transvaal in 1890 as a hawker. He opened a business in Johannesburg and Pretoria 1893. Although of modest education he became a very effective *sayagrahi*. He delivered an ardent speech of resistance in the Pretoria mosque on 31 July 1907. He became Chairman of the British Indian Association from September 1908 in succession to Essop Mia. On 20 January 1909 he wrote a letter to the press advocating that merchants dissolve their businesses to free them for *satyagraha* but only one other person followed him. He was arrested before he was due to leave for London. To keep *satyagraha* going he and Gandhi addressed a rally in April 1913.

Campbell-Bannerman, Henry (1836-1908) Born Henry Campbell in Glasgow, educated at Glasgow University and Trinity College, Cambridge. His father was a Lord Provost of Glasgow. He added his mother's name in 1872. Liberal MP for Stirling from 1868. Ministerial positions from 1871. Leader of the Liberal Party from 1899. He at first supported the Anglo-Boer War but later condemned the "methods of barbarism" being used by the British. He became Prime Minister in 1905 when Balfour resigned and in January 1906 the Liberals were returned with a large majority. His Government granted self-government to the Transvaal and Orange Free State. He remained in post until shortly before his death.

Cartwright, Albert (1868-1956) Born in Lancashire, he became assistant editor of the Johannesburg *Star* in 1892 and was editor of *South African News,* a liberal Cape Town daily, 1899-1905. He was imprisoned for criticising martial law and was a supporter of the Indian cause. He was editor of the *Transvaal Leader* 1907-11. Gandhi and Cartwright became friends from 1906. He was a member of the Progressive Party. He participated in the negotiations about the Black Act which led to the compromise of voluntary registration and was shocked when Smuts reneged. He attended a reception with the Gandhis at Hotel Cecil in London on 8 August 1914.

Churchill, Winston S. (1874-1965) Followed his father Randolph into politics and was a Liberal MP 1900-23, including First Lord of the Admiralty 1911-15, Secretary of War 1918-21, Colonial Secretary 1921-2. He changed party and was Conservative Chancellor of the Exchequer 1924-29. He was out of the Cabinet until 1939. He became Prime Minister of the Coalition Government 1940-5. In spite of his fame as a war leader his Party was defeated by Labour in 1945, but became again Prime Minister 1951-5. Churchill and Gandhi met only once, in 1906 when Churchill was Under Secretary for the Colonies and pointed out to Gandhi that legislative decisions would soon be devolved. As an imperialist Churchill was opposed to independence for India. Perhaps his most notorious description of Gandhi was uttered when the latter met Viceroy Lord Irwin: "It is alarming and also nauseating to see Mr Gandhi, a seditious Middle Temple lawyer [actually Inner Temple], now posing as a fakir of a type well known in the East, striding half-naked up the steps of the vice-regal palace, while he is still organising and conducting a defiant campaign of civil disobedience, to parley on equal terms with the representative of the King-Emperor."

Desai, Mahadev (1892-42) Gandhi's principal secretary from 1918 until his death in 1942. Gandhi and he first met in Ahmedabad in September 1917. Son of a village school teacher, he became a translator and then qualified in law but made little money and became an inspector of farming cooperatives in the villages around Ahmedabad. He proved to be the perfect secretary for Gandhi – intelligent, a fine translator, industrious, totally committed. He kept a diary throughout his period as secretary and wrote a number of books about the independence movement. He accompanied Gandhi to London in 1931 and joined Gandhi in prison in 1932. He died of a heart attack in prison with Gandhi in the Aga Khan's Palace in Poona in 1942.

Despard, Charlotte (1844-1939) Suffragist, pacifist, socialist. Born Charlotte French (her younger brother John became Field Marshal Lord French). Married an Anglo-Irishman, Maximilian Despard, in 1870. She had several novels published. After Max died in 1890 she started to involve herself in public activities. She became a Roman Catholic but her religious beliefs were very eclectic and she was also attracted to Theosophy. She became a member of both the Independent Labour Party and the Social Democratic Federation. She was the principal founder in 1908 of the Women's Freedom League which was a moderate break-away from the Women's' Social and Political Union of which she had been joint-secretary since 1906 (imprisoned in Holloway in 1907). In 1918 she became President of the London Vegetarian Society. In 1921 she moved to Ireland and in 1926 she supported the Irish Workers' Party. In 1932 she campaigned for de Valera who won the election. She supported the republican cause in Spain.

Doctor, Jayakunvar Manilal Also known as 'Jeki'. She was the daughter of Dr Pranjivan Mehta and married an Indian Mauritian and barrister, Manilal Doctor, who arrived in Durban on October 1911 having been at the Indian National Congress in India where he was party to Polak's resolution to abolish the system of indentured labour. He left for Fiji in July 1912 but his 20 year old wife remained at Tolstoy Form helping with the school. She moved to Phoenix with the Gandhis in 1913 and had an affair with Manilal Gandhi. She went to prison with Kasturba during the 1913 campaign. She later joined her husband in Fiji.

Doke, Rev. Joseph J. (1861-1913) His father was a Baptist minister in Devon. Joseph went to South Africa in 1882 and returned to Britain in 1885 by way of India. He married Agnes Biggs and they had 3 sons and a daughter. He ministered in Bristol, New Zealand and Grahamstown, South Africa, before going to the Central Baptist Church, Johannesburg in 1907. He was concerned with temperance, gambling and sexual morality (drunkenness and prostitution were major problems there), and also advocated a union of non-conformist churches. In late 1907 he went to see Gandhi at his office as he was curious about him and saw Sonja Schlesin typing in the outer office. On 12 January 1908 he preached a sermon expressing the view that the Asians had imbibed the teachings of Jesus. On the morning of 10 February, Doke went to the Registry Office in case there was trouble and found Gandhi on the floor being treated by a doctor. He had been attacked by Mir Alam Khan. Doke then took him by carriage to his home where he was nursed by his wife and himself. Gandhi had 5 stitches in his cheek and lip and stayed in the Doke household for 10 days. Later on, the Dokes' daughter Olive, who sang 'Lead Kindly Light' for Gandhi during his recuperation, taught Ramdas singing. On 14 March a dinner was held by the Indian community for those who had supported them. Mrs Doke was given a fine oak desk in appreciation. During 1908 Doke wrote the first biography of Gandhi, *An Indian Patriot in South Africa,* which was addressed to the British public. It was published in October 1909 in about 700 copies. In the second half of 1909 Doke acted as editor of *Indian Opinion* while Gandhi was in Britain and Polak in India. In 1912 he opposed conscription for the armed forces of South Africa. In July 1913, Doke, along with his youngest son Clement (20), went on a missionary journey north as far as northern Rhodesia but he died of a fever on 15 August. Gandhi was invited to take part in the memorial service for him on 24 August.

Dube, John L. (1871-1946) A Zulu, his father was a Congregational minister and his son managed to get an education in the USA 1887-92 particularly at Oberlin College, Ohio, a liberal arts college which admitted both blacks and women. He was an admirer of Booker T. Washington who believed that blacks could raise their status through education and hard work. He became a school teacher on his return to South Africa. He established in 1901 a rural commune north of Durban, which included a school and craft centre, called the Ohlange Institute. He published from there *Ilanga Lase Natal* (*The Rising Sun*) from April 1903. He wrote the first historical novel in Zulu. Gandhi first met him in 1905 at a meeting of the British Association for the Advancement of Science which was being held in South Africa. He founded the Natal Native Congress and later the South African Native National Congress of which he was the first President in 1912. It later developed into the African National Congress. In 1914 he led a deputation to Britain against the Native Land Act. He remained a moderate in politics.

Elgin, Lord, Victor Alexander Bruce, 9th Earl (1849-1917) Educated at Eton and Baliol College, Oxford. Viceroy of India 1894-99 (his father was also Viceroy and died in India). In 1905 he was appointed Colonial Secretary by Prime Minister Campbell-Bannerman.

Gandhi, Chhaganlal (b.1880) Mohandas' nephew, brother of Maganlal. He worked as a clerk in Bombay and moved his family, wife Kashiben and young child, into Mohandas Gandhi's bungalow in Santa Cruz, Bombay when Gandhi left for South Africa. They came to South Africa in 1904 and he was a founder member of Phoenix Settlement. He helped Albert West with the production, accounts and distribution of

Indian Opinion. He also taught arithmetic in the Phoenix school. From 1908 he edited the Gujarati section and kept accounts. He was sent to Britain in 1911 to study law (paid for by Dr Mehta) but fell ill and returned to stay at Phoenix until Gandhi left South Africa. He was imprisoned at the same time as the women *satyagrahis* in 1913. He later settled in India at Sabarmati Ashram.

Gandhi, Devadas (1900-1957) Youngest son of Kasturba and Mohandas, he was delivered by his father in Durban. Staying at Sabarmati Ashram in 1920 after evening prayers he used to give well-informed commentaries on the daily newspapers. When Motilal Nehru's *Independent* was forced to close down Devadas produced a hand written version at Allahabad. He led the non-cooperation movement in the city and was imprisoned. He was sent by his father to ascertain the facts of the Chauri Chaura massacre of policemen which occurred on 8 February 1921 and his report led Gandhi to abandon the *satyagraha*. Although Devadas had little formal education he was very well informed. In London for the Second Round Table Conference he met George Bernard Shaw who called him Mahatma Minor. He married Lakshmi the daughter of Rajagopalachari, one of the leading figures in the Indian National Congress, in 1927. It was an intercaste marriage and was opposed by the orthodox Hindus. In 1932 he visited the North West Frontier Province and reported to his father on the severe treatment of the Khudai Khidmatgar movement founded by Abdul Ghaffar Khan. He became editor of the *Hindustan Times* and became chairman of the World Editors' Conference. According to Pyarelal he was a man of exceptional good temper and good judgement. In 1957 while taking proofs of Pyarelal's *Mahatma Gandhi: The Last Phase* with a view to serialisation in the *Hindustan Times* he had a fatal heart attack.

Gandhi, Harilal (1888-1948) Harilal went with his parents and Manilal to South Africa in 1896. His father and Chhaganlal gave him some teaching. In India in 1901 he went to school while staying with Gandhi's sister in Rajkot. When the family returned to South Africa in 1905 Harilal stayed behind with an uncle so that he could go to school. He fell in love with Gulab (or Chanchi) the daughter of Gandhi's friend Haridas Vora and became engaged. Harilal and Chanchi married in 1906 (without his parents' knowledge) and came to Phoenix in 1907. Harilal worked at first in his father's office in Johannesburg and then helped with the press at Phoenix. Chanchi arrived later and was pregnant. Their first child was born in April 1908. On 28 July 1908

Harilal was tried for hawking without a licence and sentenced to 7 days' hard labour, the first of several imprisonments. On 10 August he was tried for not having a registration certificate to enter the Transvaal. He received a six month sentence. He fasted while in prison in protest against the poor prison diet. He became known as Gandhi Junior. But when Gandhi asked Manilal and others to become celibate Harilal began to question some of his father's actions. He also wanted to study for the bar but his father did not support him in this. When Dr Mehta offered to pay for one of Gandhi's sons' studies and Gandhi then proposed Chhaganlal instead, Harilal was resentful. While Harilal was in prison Chanchi went to India where her second child was born in January 1911. In May 1911 Harilal disappeared. He had gone to Delagoa Bay but did not have money for the ship to India. Here he was recognised and Kallenbach went and brought him back to Phoenix. Unreconciled, his father arranged for him to go to India. Being recognised in Zanzibar he was given an address of welcome and replied in support of *satyagraha*. He took up study but failed exams at the end of 1912 and took a job. When his parents arrived back in India in 1915 he met them and spent much time with them but in March 1916 decided to part company. He tried to establish himself in business in Calcutta and the family were happy for a period until he lost his job and he sent his family to Rajkot. In 1918 a son died and shortly after Chanchi died also of influenza. This was a devastating blow to Harilal. He was left to bring up three children and Gandhi insisted he should marry a widow, leading to another break between them. He began to disintegrate. He was unsuccessful in any career and became an alcoholic. In 1935 Harilal briefly converted to Islam. He was late for his father's funeral and died the next year.

Gandhi, Kasturba (1869-1944) She and Mohandas were married at 13, Gandhi left to study in Britain in 1888 and did not return to India until 1891. She and Mohandas along with Harilal and Manilal left for South Africa in November 1896 (Gandhi's second period there). Ramdas was born in 1898 and Devadas in 1900. When the family returned to India in 1901 Gandhi asked his wife to give away gifts given to her by the Indian community and she resented this. Gandhi returned to South Africa in December 1902. Kasturba and the three younger sons returned to South Africa at the beginning of 1905. In 1906 her husband announced that he was now celibate. Kasturba was ill in 1908 when her husband was in prison. She joined the final phase of *satyagraha* when Indian marriages were not being legally recognised. She was one of the pioneer group of 12 men and 4 women who left Phoenix to cross into Transvaal at Volksrust on 15 September 1913. She was arrested ad deported back into Natal and on a second attempt was imprisoned in Pietermaritzburg 23 September to 22 December 1913. She left with Gandhi for London and then India in 1914. She was self-effacing, had little education, and was a loyal support to her demanding husband, although she did on occasion assert herself. She died in prison in the presence of Mohandas on 22 February 1944 during the Quit India campaign.

Gandhi, Maganlal (1883-1928) Younger brother of Chhaganlal, sons of a cousin of Mohandas Gandhi, Khushaldas – brought up by Gandhi's parents. Going with Gandhi to South Africa in late 1902 he became a storekeeper with a cousin in Tongaat near Durban. Like his brother he was a founder member of Phoenix where they lived with their families, Maganlal followed Gandhi in becoming celibate while married. He did gardening and carpentry and had a practical bent and was very committed to Gandhi and his ideals. He helped to coin the word *'satyagraha'* by suggesting *'sadagraha'* meaning firmness in a good cause. He became essential to the running of Phoenix and did not take part in *satygraha* for that reason. After Gandhi's and his return to India Maganlal managed the ashrams at Ahmedabad but almost left after his wife opposed the admission of an untouchable family. He also promoted hand-made cloth, *khadi*. He could be severe but Gandhi greatly admired his dedication. He died suddenly of pneumonia while visiting Champaran.

Gandhi, Manilal (1892-1956) The second son of Mohandas Gandhi. He came with his family to South Africa at the start of 1897. He was arrested twice in 1910 and got 20 days in prison. In July 1913 he fell in love and had an affair with Jeki Doctor, who was married, at Phoenix and as a consequence his father fasted for one week. He was imprisoned for 3 months in 1913 after arrest at Volksrust. He left with his parents in 1914 for India but returned in 1916 to Phoenix. From 1916 he edited the Gujarati section of *Indian Opinion* and from 1920 to 1955 he was the general editor. In 1927 he married Sushila Mashruwala in India. In 1929 he returned to India and joined the 1930 Salt Satyagraha where he was badly beaten at Dharasana and then given a one year prison sentence. In 1931 he returned to South Africa. On one occasion he took his daughter Sita on the lower deck of a bus, this deck being reserved for whites and he broke the laws of separate facilities often.

In 1945 he spent one year with his father in India. In 1946 he was sentenced to one month's imprisonment for participating in the passive resistance campaign in Durban. He was a strong opponent of *apartheid* but held that nonviolence was the way to eliminate it. He was imprisoned in 1952 for opposing the pass laws. He died on 8 April 1956 after suffering a stroke.

Gandhi, Prabhudas (1901-95) Son of Chhaganlal and Kashi. He wrote an account of his childhood at Phoenix between 1904 and 1914, *My Childhood with Gandhiji.*

Gandhi, Ramdas (1898-1969) The third son of Mohandas and Kasturba, he was born in Durban. He was taken to India in 1901 where they stayed in Rajkot until the family moved to Bombay, but at the end of 1902 they returned to South Africa. His education was irregular but at different times he studied with Vinoba Bhave who taught him Mathematics and Sanskrit, and C. F. Andrews who taught him English. He also studied music and was a good singer. He went to Shantiniketan in 1914 with the Phoenix settlers. When at Kochrab Ashram (near Ahmedabad) admission of an untouchable family drove Gandhi's sister away which upset Ramdas who was close to her. He returned with Manilal to South Africa partly because of his poor health in India. Here he took up a succession of jobs in the clothing industry. He returned to India in 1921 for the Congress session at Ahmedabad, and in 1923 he saw Harilal who had a business in Calcutta but observed he was unwise with his money. In the following years he promoted *khadi* and in 1928 he married Nirmala, daughter of Dr Haridas Vora. He joined Vallabhbhai Patel in the Bardoli Satyagraha where he became manager of the Bardoli ashram which involved feeding sometimes as many as 250 people and nursing the sick. During the Salt Satyagraha he was leader of a group at Surat and in March 1930 was given a 6 month sentence, which gave him the opportunity to study. After the Second Round Table Conference he was put in Yeravda prison where there were over 2,000 *satyagrahis.* He was never robust and imprisonment weakened his health. Jamnalal Bajaj, a wealthy Gandhian, gave him the job of manager of Khadi Bhandar in Wardha and later he sold cloth in Bombay. When Kallenbach came to India Ramdas decided to go back with him to South Africa in 1937 where he looked after *Indian Opinion* while Manilal went to India but his health did not improve and he returned to India. During this period Nirmala studied in India. He took up work with Tata Oil Mill Co. and later became manager of the Nagpur Depot. Their home became an extension of Sevagram and many visitors were looked after by Nirmala and Ramdas. He retired in 1951 and they settled in Sevagram. Ramdas died in Bombay in 1969.

Gandhi-Dhupelia, Sita (1928-1999) Eldest daughter of Manilal and Sushila Gandhi. In her teenage years, from 1943, she lived in India and got to know her grandfather. In 1946 she entered Benares Hindu University. She returned to South Africa in 1948 but was unable to enter higher education in South Africa as her Indian qualifications were not recognised. She helped with the production of *Indian Opinion,* as manager and sub-editor, and in 1950 helped to produce a special edition celebrating India's transition to a republic. In 1951 she and her parents several times entered the European part of Durban Municipal Library in protest at the segregated facility but she was disappointed that they were not arrested. Sita married Shashikant Dhupelia in 1953 and they settled in Durban where she started nursing but gave it up to look after their three children. She continued to help with *Indian Opinion.*

Gandhi, Sushila (1907-88) She married Manilal in 1927. Her father, N. Mashruwala, was a wealthy land-owner, and his brother Kishorelal was a close associate of Mohandas. They had three children – Sita, Arun, Ela. She learned type-setting and edited the Gujarati version of *Indian Opinion* and after her husband's illness she edited the paper from 1955 to 1961 with the help of her daughter Sita and others.

Gokhale, Gopal Krishna (1866-1915) Born in Maharashtra, he became a school teacher. He was a founder of Ferguson College in Poona in 1885. He was elected to the Bombay Legislative Council in 1899. In 1902 he resigned as Professor of History and Political Economy to devote more time to politics and public affairs and became a member of the Imperial Legislature. In 1905 he founded the Servants of India Society, the members of which took a vow of poverty and service. He was elected President of the Indian National Congress in 1905. Although a moderate reformer he recognised the exceptional qualities of the more radical Gandhi and in turn Gandhi had the greatest respect for him. Gandhi was attracted by his spirit of service and devotion to truth. He came to South Africa in late 1912 to help the Indian community but was too ready to take Smuts and Botha at their word, which was not borne out by experience.

Habib, Hajee Born in Porbander, as was Gandhi, he arrived in South

Africa in 1880 to be manager of Dada & Co. which his brother owned. He was a founding member of the Natal Indian Congress in 1894. He gave an emotional and powerful speech in Gujarati (with some interpolations in English for the benefit of the press) at the 1906 meeting attended by Muslims, Hindus and Christians. He became Chairman of the British India Association and was secretary of the Pretoria mosque. He left the Transvaal in December 1907. He travelled to London with Gandhi in 1909 but he withdrew his support, along with most of the merchant elite, after 1909.

Hosken, William (1851-1925) He was born in Cornwall and came to South Africa in 1874. There he became manager of a gold mine and was associated with the 1895 Jameson Raid for which he was sentenced to two years' imprisonment. In 1902 he was appointed to the first Johannesburg Town Council and in 1903 elected to the Transvaal Legislative Council for the Progressive Party which represented mainly mine owners. He was an active Methodist also. He was a liberal in race relations. In April 1903 he promoted a petition against new restrictions on Indian residence and trade. He often represented Indians and Africans to white bodies. He founded in 1908 the Committee of European Sympathisers of the Satyagraha Movement.

Isaac, Gabriel (d.1914) A jeweller by profession. An observant Jew and a vegetarian. He collected subscriptions for *Indian Opinion*. In 1908 he offered to become nominal owner of Indian shops owned by those who did not take out registration certificates. In July 1909 he went to Delagoa Bay to help those being deported to India. In 1913 during the final phase of *satyagraha* he was imprisoned.

Jinnah, Mohammed Ali (1876-1948) He was born in Karachi to a prosperous business family. After attending the University of Bombay he studied for the bar at Lincoln's Inn, London, from 1895. His wife died while he was in the UK. He campaigned for Dadabai Naoroji (first Asian member of Parliament) and then returned to India. He joined Congress in 1906 and was nominated to the Legislative Council in 1907. He joined the Muslim League in 1913 (it had formed in 1906) and became President of the League in 1916. He encouraged co-operation between the League and the Congress. He married a Parsi, Ruttenbai, against her parents' wishes; she died at only 29 in 1929. Disputes in the League then drove him to settle in London and practise law there 1930-35. He was asked to return to India and become President of the League but in the elections of 1937 the League did not do well and Congress did not wish to share power. In 1940 the League opted to campaign for a separate state. During the 1940s Hindu/Muslim positions became polarised with periodic communal violence and Britain decided to opt for separation into Pakistan and India. Jinnah became the First Governor General of Pakistan 1947.

Kallenbach, Hermann (1871-1945) He came from Lithuania/Russia, father a timber merchant, and he was educated in German schools and then studied architecture in Stuttgart. He went to South Africa in 1896 and practised as an architect. He was introduced to Gandhi in 1903 by advocate R. K. Khan and they gradually developed a close relationship. In 1910 he bought a farm 21 miles from Johannesburg and named it Tolstoy Farm, having been greatly impressed by the mature Tolstoy, and gave it to Gandhi for *satyagrahis*. In July 1910 he learned sandal making at Marianhill Monastery near Durban and taught it at Tolstoy Farm, to Gandhi and others, as well as carpentry and gardening. He visited Britain in 1911 and met the writer Edward Carpenter and translators of Tolstoy's works, Aylmer Maude and Isabella Fyvie Mayo. He and Gandhi gave up milk in 1912. In September 1912 he was made a Trustee of Phoenix. At the beginning of 1913 the Tolstoy Farm experiment came to an end, but Kallenbach left it reluctantly. Most of settlers went to Phoenix. He was particularly active in the final phase of *satyagraha* – in prison 10 November to 18 December 1913. He looked after the arrangements at Volksrust at the time of the Great March. He left South Africa with Gandhi but was imprisoned in the UK (Isle of Man) as an alien due to the war and did not get to India. 1918-20 he visited his family in East Prussia. He returned to South Africa to pursue his career as an architect but he also re-established links with Phoenix and former colleagues. In 1922 he intentionally travelled by train from Phoenix to Durban in a compartment for non-European and refused to leave. He kept in touch with Manilal and Sushila Gandhi. In 1923 he assisted his family to emigrate from Germany to South Africa. In 1937 he visited Palestine, and then at last visited Gandhi at Sevagram, returning in 1939 but he fell ill on the second occasion. He died on 25 March 1945 in Johannesburg. He left the greater part of his estate to Jewish settlers in Palestine.

Kaur, Rajkumari Amrit (d.1964) A princess, she was educated at Oxford and was introduced to Gandhi by Gokhale at the Bombay Congress of 1915. The family were Christian and had many contacts with Raj officials. She joined Gandhi at Wardha in 1934 where she learned spinning and scavenging. She was imprisoned during the Quit India movement and the conditions badly affected her health. She helped with the production of *Harijan* and occasionally with negotiatons such as the Cabinet Mission of 1946. After independence she was Minister of Health for 10 years.

Kitchen, Herbert (d.1915) He was the nephew of a Dean of Durham but became a theosophist and founded with Ritch a theosophical society in Johannesburg in 1899. Gandhi came there in 1903 and got to know all the members. Kitchen became a part of Gandhi's household at Beach Grove Villa, Durban. During the Anglo-Boer War he was a volunteer in the Engineering Corps and sent Gandhi descriptions of his observations in areas cleared of Boers while Gandhi worked with the ambulance corps. Kitchen gave up his profession of electrical engineer to join Phoenix. He edited the English edition of *Indian Opinion* in 1906. At Phoenix he had a large room for experiments with X-rays and radio and he also had a large library. He set up lights in the settlement. After he left Phoenix Gandhi and his family used this room. Unfortunately he had a bad temper and was also addicted to alcohol. He resigned from Phoenix as he disagreed with passive resistance and in 1915 he shot himself after a business failure.

Lajput Rai, Lala (1865-1928) A fiery orator from the Punjab. He studied law in Lahore. He joined the Congress and also became a leading figure in Arya Samaj, which promoted a conservative Hinduism. He spent WWI in the USA and on return he presided over a special session of Congress in Calcutta in September 1920 which adopted *satyagraha* for self-government. He and Nehru were opposed to Gandhi's abandoning *satyagraha* over the violence by nominal supporters at Chauri Chaura. He did not approve of the Khilafat movement which Gandhi supported after WWI. He was in prison 1921-3 and then became deputy leader of the Swaraj Party formed in 1923 by Motilal Nehru and C. R. Das to wreck the dyarchical constitution. In 1923 he was elected to the legislative assembly and advocated a boycott of the Simon Commission in 1928. During a demonstration he was assaulted by a British officer and died a few days later.

Ligt, Bart de (1883-1938) Dutch anarchist and pacifist. He studied theology at Utrecht, joined in 1909 the Union of Christian Socialists, and took up the pastorate of the church at Nuenen, the same church of which Van Gogh's father had been pastor. He was imprisoned for his opposition to WWI and on release was banned from certain parts of the country. In 1918 he married Catherina who was also a strong pacifist. He was imprisoned again in 1921 for organising a general strike in support of a conscientious objector. He was a prolific writer. His approach was utopian – the transformation of the whole of society – but one that was very self-aware and practical. His biography of Erasmus was published in 1936. *The Conquest of Violence: an Essay on War and Revolution* 1937 deals with nonviolent action as a substitute for war. He felt Gandhi was inconsistent in his pacifism.

Magnes, Rabbi Judah (1877-1948) Jewish pacifist. Born in California, he was a good baseball player as well as academically able. At 17 he entered the Reform Seminary in Cincinnati. He opposed the Spanish American War of 1898. He had to leave his first two posts as rabbi partly due to his outspoken Zionism but also because of his relatively conservative form of Judaism in Reform congregations. He was a staunch pacifist during WWI. His pacifism was rooted in traditional Jewish reverence for life. In 1923 he settled in Palestine and helped establish the Hebrew University of which he became the first Chancellor. He was opposed to a purely Jewish state and hoped for a shared state with the Palestinians. He reluctantly abandoned pacifism in the face of persecution by the Nazis. He died on a visit to the USA.

Mehta, Dr. Pranjivan J. (1858-1932) A medical doctor (who also read for the bar) who met Gandhi when a student in London and they remained life-long friends. Gandhi had an insurance policy with Mehta's brother which he cancelled out of principle in 1909. Dr Mehta moved to Rangoon where he started a nationalist paper. When in London in 1909 to place his son in a British boarding school he met up with Gandhi. From then on he made funds available to Phoenix. He donated substantially to Gandhi's causes in India also. His daughter Jayakunvar M. Doctor stayed at Phoenix from 1911-1913.

Morley, Lord, John (1838-1923) His father was a surgeon, and he was educated at Lincoln College, Oxford. He became an editor and political biographer. He was elected Liberal MP for Newcastle-on-Tyne in 1883. He was Secretary of State for India 1905-10, being made a Viscount in 1908, and resigning from Government in 1914. The Morley-Minto reforms (Minto being Viceroy) in 1909 gave an increased elected element to the Indian legislatures.

Murray, Gilbert (1866-1957) Classical scholar and humanist. Born in Australia, educated at St John's College, Oxford. Professor of Greek at Glasgow University at only 23, he spent most of his career at Oxford. Famed for his translations of Greek dramatists and poets. He was President of the League of Nations Union 1923-38 and was one of the founders of Oxfam. Gandhi met Murray in 1914 and Murray wrote an article on Gandhi in *The Hibbert Journal* (January 1918). He was one of a group of academics who quizzed Gandhi at Oxford in 1931.

Naidoo, Thambi A Tamil from Mauritius, who knew Hindi also. He was a small trader. He became one of the most committed *satyagrahis* and was arrested many times. The 1907 voluntary registration document was signed by him as well as Gandhi and Quinn. He raised money from Johannesburg Tamils in 1907. Like Gandhi he was assaulted when voluntarily registering. On 13 October 1913 there was a public meeting in Newcastle mining area over the £3 tax which was led by Naidoo who was accompanied by several women in addition to men. The next day a party including eleven women and six children tried to bring workers out on strike. He was arrested but released. After addressing 78 workers at Farleigh Colliery they struck. The strike soon involved 2000 in Northern Natal and this doubled within a week. On 29 October Gandhi led 200 strikers and their families out of Newcastle towards the Transvaal border. Then a party of 300 led by Naidoo set out. His son also participated.

Naidu, Sarojini (1879-1949) Her father Chattopadhyay was Principal of Nizam's College, Hyderabad. She entered Madras University aged 12 and then went to King's College London and Girton College Cambridge. She married M. G. Naidu, principal medical officer to the Nizam of Hyderabad, in 1899 and they had 2 sons and 2 daughters. She first met Gandhi in London in 1914. In 1924 she visited east and south Africa. She was elected President of the Congress in 1925, and toured the USA 1928-9 on behalf of Congress. She was one of the leaders of the Salt Satyagraha 1930 and was in London for the Second Round Table Conference 1931. She was imprisoned in 1930, 1932 and 1942. Governor of United Provinces 1947. She wrote poetry, in English, for which she was well known in India.

Naoroji, Dadabhai (1825-1917) Born into a Parsi family near Bombay, his father was a Zoroastrian priest who died when his son was only four. He was educated at Elphinstone College in Bombay where he became a mathematics teacher in 1845, and in 1852 a full Professor at the College, the first Indian to hold such a position. In 1855 he sailed for Britain to set up an export/import business with two brothers. He began to develop an interest in politics, both British and Indian, and built up an expertise in the economics of the Raj and demonstrated how Britain drained India of wealth. Another of his concerns was the entry conditions for Indians to the Indian Civil Service. He became the first Indian to be elected an MP, Liberal for Holborn 1892-5. He moved between both countries and represented the Indian National Congress in Britain, and was its President in 1886, 1891 and 1905. He was a moderate reformer, but refused a knighthood, and became known as the Grand Old Man of India.

Nayar, Dr. Sushila (1914-2001) Born in west Punjab, now in Pakistan, she became physician to Gandhi, and also trained paramedical staff for village work. She accompanied Gandhi in Noakhali during communal disturbances in 1947. She took further medical training in the USA after Gandhi's death. Entering parliament in 1957 she was Minister of Health 1962-7. In her later career she concentrated on community and rural health. She was involved with many medical organisations and also founded Kasturba Hospital at Sevagram. She completed the huge biography of Gandhi begun by her brother **Pyarelal** (1899-1982) who was principal secretary to Gandhi after Mahadev's death.

Nehru, Jawaharlal (1889-1964) From a family of Kashmiri Brahmins, but born in Allahabad. Father **Motilal** (1861-1931) was a successful barrister. Jawaharlal, after private tutoring, went at 15 to Harrow school and then Trinity College, Cambridge. He studied natural science and then law; returning to Allahabad he married Kamala in 1916, Indira being born the following year. Both father and son became involved in the independence movement from 1919 and Jawaharlal became a socialist in the 1920s. He was President of Congress at Lahore in 1929. Kamala died in Switzerland in 1936. Jawaharlal became close to Gandhi although he did not follow Gandhi's decentralised and village-based approach nor his principled nonviolence. He spent a total of 9 years in prison, the longest being 1942-5. He became India's first Prime Minister, believing in a secular, democratic socialist polity. He also tried to follow a non-aligned foreign policy but Kashmir remained a problem and soured relations with Pakistan, Portuguese Goa was taken over in 1961, and a brief war with China broke out in 1962.

Pankhurst, Emmeline (1858-1928) Leading suffragette. Emmeline Gouldon married Richard Pankhurst, barrister, socialist and feminist, in 1879. She became a Poor Law Guardian. In 1889 the Pankhursts founded the Women's Franchise League, and in 1894 they joined the Independent Labour Party. After her husband's death she opened a shop in Manchester. Finding that even many socialists were not in favour of female franchise she founded the Social and Political Union for Women's Suffrage, which only women could join, in 1903. In 1905 she led the movement in a more militant direction. She was supported by her daughters **Christabel** (1880-1958), an outstanding public speaker who qualified in law although she could not practise, **Sylvia** (1882-1960), who was an artist and socialist, and **Adela**, also a socialist. All spent time in jail. Emmeline and Christabel were ardent supporters of the war while Sylvia was a pacifist. In 1918 many women over the age of 30 were given the vote and Christabel stood for Parliament but was not elected. After WWI Emmeline joined the Conservative Party, Christabel became a Christian evangelist, while Sylvia remained a committed socialist.

Pearson, Rev. William Winstanley (d.1923) He went as a missionary to Bengal where he met Charlie Andrews but had to return to the UK because of poor health. Andrews met him again in London in 1912 and persuaded him to return to India where he took up a job as tutor to the son of Lala Sultan Singh. At Gokhale's request they both went to South Africa to meet Gandhi in 1914. Pearson visited indentured labourers and also Africans in the vicinity of Phoenix. He met John Dube at the Inanda Institute and suggested that Africans take up *satyagraha* but Dube expressed the view that Africans would retaliate under provocation and could not control their temper as well as the Indians. He left South Africa with Andrews in February 1914 and went to Tagore's Shantiniketan where he did some teaching. Both then accompanied Tagore on a tour of Japan. They then both went to Fiji to investigate the conditions of labourers there. In 1923 on his way back to India after a considerable absence Pearson was killed in a railway accident in Italy.

Pethick-Lawrence, Emmeline (1867-1964) From a well-to-do family. She worked in a west London mission 1890-1895. She married **Frederick Lawrence** (1871-1961), who was also concerned with issues of poverty, in 1901 and they decided to use both surnames as an egalitarian gesture. They opposed the Government over the Anglo-Boer War and visited

South Africa in 1905, becoming friends with Olive Schreiner. They both became active in the women's suffrage movement after Keir Hardie introduced them to Emmeline Pankhurst. Emmeline became Treasurer of the Women's Social and Political Union but they did not go along with the increasing militancy of the WSPU and were expelled by Emmeline and Christabel Pankhurst. Frederick became Labour MP for East Leicester from 1923-31. He was elected again in 1935, and from 1945-47, now in the Lords, he was Secretary of State for India. In March 1946 he was one of three Ministers forming the Cabinet Mission to India.

Phillips, Rev. Charles White pastor of Ebenezer Congregational Church (1896-1937) with a large Cape Coloured congregation which had mission stations throughout the Rand. He was a strong supporter of the Indian cause. He wrote to the Lt. Governor protesting about the Town Council's decision to exclude Coloureds from riding with Whites on trams. He organised a campaign against the Government-promoted opium trade in the Transvaal. He had a considerable knowledge of the various ethnic groups in the country and in spite of supporting civil disobedience he remained on good terms with more traditional whites. His **wife** was at one time Acting Chairman of the European Sympathisers Committee and she also unveiled the memorial stone to Valliamma Munusamy in Braamfontein Cemetery just before Gandhi left South Africa in 1914.

Polak, Henry Salomon Leon (1882-1959) Born in Dover, educated in London and Switzerland. He went to South Africa 1903. Polak was sub-editor of the *Transvaal Critic,* an anti-Indian paper, when he and Gandhi met in 1904. On marriage the Polaks lived in the Gandhi household for a couple of years. They moved to Phoenix for a little while in 1906 and Henry became editor of *Indian Opinion* following Kitchen. He became Assistant Secretary of the Transvaal British Indian Association in 1906. Polak became articled to Gandhi after Ritch left for Britain and was enrolled as an attorney in 1908. The BIA paid his expenses for defending *satyagrahis* for free. In 1909 Polak went to India to spread the South African Indian cause and stayed for a year. He addressed many meetings, met Gokhale, and had two short writings published – one on the South African situation and a brief biography of Gandhi. He went again 1911-12 during which the Indian National Congress passed a resolution concerning abolition of the indentured labour system. He was arrested during the Great March in 1913 and imprisoned 17 September to 18 December. The Polaks stayed on in

South Africa on Gandhi's departure in December 1913. During 1916-17 the Polaks were in India but Henry became seriously ill and returned to Britain. Millie left India with the children in 1919 and Henry set up in law practice. Henry helped with Gandhi's arrangements during his visit for the Round Table Conference 1931 although he had become more conservative by then and had been supporting the Commonwealth of India League founded by Annie Besant. Henry had a serious disagreement with Gandhi over the Quit India movement during WWII.

Polak, Maud Sister of Henry Polak. She helped the 1909 delegation in London. In August she visited, with Gandhi, Habib and Dr Mehta, the Tolstoyan community at Whiteway in the Cotswolds. She and her sister Sally wanted to join the Phoenix settlement but were dissuaded by Millie Polak who told them that the conditions there were too primitive. Maud worked as the Secretary of the South African British Indian Committee in London after Ritch returned to South Africa in 1911. She also gave office help, now as Mrs Cheesman, during the 1931 visit of Gandhi to London.

Polak, Millie Graham (c1880-1962) Millie Downs married Henry Polak in Johannesburg 1905. They had met in London at the South Place Ethical Society. She helped to educate the Gandhi boys, and they had themselves two sons, Waldo and Leon (or Brownie). She was a founder of the Transvaal Indian Women's Association. When Henry went to India in 1909 she returned to Britain with the children for two years. She went to India in 1911 with Henry. She wrote her first-hand account of Gandhi in South Africa from notes taken at the time and published them as *Mr Gandhi: The Man* 1931. She died 5 May 1962.

Quinn, Leung Many Chinese in the Transvaal were indentured labourers in the gold mines. Quinn was Chairman of the Chinese Association. The Chinese sent a delegation to London in 1906 to oppose the enactment of the Black Act requiring registration with finger prints of all Asians over 8 years of age. In 1907 they joined Indians in opposition to the Black Act, 900 taking an oath of resistance. Gandhi was very impressed by their solidarity. Only 8% of Asians registered. Quinn was present at the bonfire of certificates at the Hamidia Mosque 16 August 1908. He spoke at meetings of Indians, and Indians spoke at meetings of Chinese. He was sent to jail in June 1909 and on his release there was a joint public meeting of Chinese and Indians.

Ritch, Louis Walter (1867-1952) He came to South Africa from Britain around 1890. He was a theosophist, a founder of the Johannesburg Lodge in 1899 which Gandhi was invited to address. He gave up his business in Transvaal to be articled to Gandhi in 1903. He nursed plague victims in Johannesburg in 1904. In 1905 he left with his wife (who had a lengthy illness) and large family for London where he trained as a barrister. He was the first Secretary of the South African British Indian Committee, set up during Gandhi's visit to London in 1906 with Lord Ampthill as Chairman, and was very active in that role of keeping British politicians informed. In 1909 he contacted Tolstoy after Tolstoy's secretary, N. N. Gusev, had been arrested and this started a short correspondence between Gandhi and the Russian. At the end of 1910 Ritch returned to Cape Town and took over Gandhi's legal firm on 15 April 1911.

Ruskin, John (1819-1900) Artist and art critic, and social philosopher. Son of a wine merchant, he was educated at Christ Church, Oxford, and travelled throughout Europe. Champion of Turner and of the Pre-Raphaelites, he also wrote on the history of architecture especially that of Venice. Slade Professor of Art, Oxford, 1869-79 and 1883-4. Turning to social issues he wrote *Unto This Last* for Cornhill Magazine in 1860, the first of many essays critical of industrial society. He believed that relationships should not be governed by harsh economics but by human standards and his social philosophy was summed up in 'there is no wealth but life'. He did not want state socialism but rather an economics which took a cooperative form; and art should be accessible to everyone since everyone needed beauty in their life. He founded the Guild of St George to demonstrate through a few practical projects how improvement in one's environment by cooperative effort would lead to a happier life.

Rustomji, Parsi (1861-1924) A Parsi merchant who came from Bombay. He was a founding member of the Natal Indian Congress in 1894. It was to his house that the Gandhis went when they disembarked at Durban in January 1897 and were met by a mob of enraged whites. He donated money to set up a small hospital with Dr Booth in charge, and also paid for the shed to house the printing press at Phoenix, and gave other financial support. As an importer he did some smuggling and was discovered and told Gandhi – Gandhi got him to confess and he was fined. As a *satyagrahi* he spent a total of 18 months in prison. He was made a Trustee of Phoenix in 1912.

Sastri, V. S. Srinivastri (1869-1946) Born in Madras, he became a teacher but his oratorical gifts led him into politics. He joined the Servants of India Society in 1907 and succeeded Gokhale as President after his death in 1915; he remained President until 1927. He entered the Indian Legislature in 1916. He passionately opposed the Rowlatt Bill in the legislative chamber after WWI. He was a moderate reformer who did not go along with the radical approach of Gandhi. He left Congress and founded the Indian Liberal Federation. He went to South Africa in 1926 and the following year he became Agent-General to look after Indian affairs there. He raised sufficiently money from Indians to establish a secondary school and teachers' training college in 1930 – Sastri College. He attended the Round Table Conference in London in 1931.

Savarkar, Vinayak (1883-1966) An Indian revolutionary from his school days in Maharashtra. While a student in London at Gray's Inn he managed a hostel for Indian students in Highgate. He inspired Indians to acts of terrorsim including the killing of Sir William Curzon-Wylie by Madanlal Dhingra a few days before Gandhi reached London on his 1909 visit (an attempt on the Viceroy Lord Curzon's life had been botched). Gandhi had visited the hostel, known as India House, on his previous visit in 1906, the year that Savarkar came to London. He wrote at this time an interpretation of the Indian Mutiny, *The Indian War of Independence of 1857*. Savarkar was involved in another assassination of an official in India and after deportation to India he was sentenced in 1910 to transportation for life to the Andaman Islands. He was however released by the Labour Government in 1924. He wrote a history of Hindu nationalism. In the 1930s he became the leader of the militant Hindu Mahasabha party. He was probably involved in the plot to assassinate Gandhi but was acquitted on lack of evidence.

Sorabji, Adajania (1883-1918) A Parsi from Bombay, he became manager of a store in Charlestown. In June 1908 he challenged the Immigrants' Restriction Act by entering the Transvaal. After a number of court appearances he was found guilty. He became a committed satyagrahi. In 1912 he went to London to study for the bar, financed by Dr Mehta, after Chhaganlal Gandhi fell ill. He was the first to enrol for the Indian ambulance unit in London during the early stages of WWI and he complained to Gandhi that the commanding officer was acting as if he was in direct command rather than Gandhi. The matter was not satisfactorily resolved. He returned to practise law in South Africa but died within a few months.

Smuts, Jan Christian (1870-1950) Soldier, lawyer, politician and philosopher. Studied law at Christ's College, Cambridge (late in life he became Chancellor of Cambridge University). He had a deep interest also in the ideas of Walt Whitman and Henri Bergson. In 1897 he started to practise law in Johannesburg and was soon made Attorney General of the South African Republic. During the Anglo-Boer War he commanded the Boer forces in Cape Colony. On the establishment of the Union of South Africa he became Minister of the Interior 1910-12 and Minister of Defence 1912-20. When gold miners struck in 1913 he used the armed forces against them, as he did on later occasions. He was Prime Minister of South Africa 1919-24, Minister of Justice 1933-39, and Prime Minister again 1939-48. In 1928 he published *Holism and Evolution*. He was a supporter of the League of Nations and he supported the Allies in both world wars and helped draft the United Nations Charter. He was defeated in 1948 by the Nationalists led by F. S. Malan. Smuts was a strong supporter of Eretz Israel and was a friend of Chaim Weitzmann.

Tagore, Rabindranath (1861-1941) Writer of novels, plays, poetry, religious works; educationalist, artist, political activist. From a distinguished Bengali family of artists and scholars. The family were active in the Hindu reform organisation, the Brahmo Samaj. He established a school at Shantiniketan in 1901 and later added an international university Visva Bharati with a strong emphasis on the arts. He was involved in the Swadeshi movement against the partition of Bengal in 1905 which included a boycott of British goods. He was awarded the Nobel Prize for Literature in 1913. Gandhi, with Andrews and Pearson, tried to reform the running of Shantiniketan along egalitarian lines when he stayed there in 1915. Tagore and Gandhi had disagreements over the years but they had a deep respect for each other.

Tolstoy, Leo (1828-1910) The Russian aristocrat and writer underwent a considerable transformation in outlook and lifestyle during his life. He was a major influence on Gandhi. He protested against pogroms, defended the Doukhobors who refused to serve in the army, and many of his writings were banned. He was excommunicated from the Orthodox Church in 1901. Of his writings the most important to Gandhi was *The Kingdom of God is Within You,* which had been sent to him by

Edward Maitland in 1893 just after it was published. Tolstoy's pared-down Christianity, emphasising the ethics of Jesus, greatly appealed to Gandhi. Tolstoy became a vegetarian and laboured on his own estates. T. M. Bondarev's concept of 'bread labour', doing some physical labour daily, which was taken up by Tolstoy, appealed greatly to Gandhi also (although he had first heard of the idea in Ruskin). Tolstoy transferred ownership of his estate to his wife and children, and advocated nonresistance, which he believed was the teaching of Jesus. Gandhi read several of Tolstoy's religious writings while in prison in 1909 and he bought some books by Tolstoy while in London that year and brought them back to Phoenix for the school. Towards the end of Tolstoy's life in 1909-10 they had an exchange of letters and Gandhi sent Tolstoy a copy of *Hind Swaraj* and Doke's biography of himself.

Vogl, E. J. William Vogl's wife. She organised sewing classes for Indian women and was involved in the Transvaal Indian Women's Association. She helped run the Indian Bazaars of 1910, 1911, 1912 and 1913 which were to raise money for those adversely affected by the civil rights campaigns.

Vogl, William M. A draper in Johannesburg. He met Gandhi in 1906. It was through Vogl and Isaac that Gandhi visited a synagogue. He and his wife later settled in Durban.

West, Ada (b.1871) Sister of Albert, settled at Phoenix in 1906 and stayed on for some time after 1914. She became known as Devibehn. She looked after the small children and kept accounts among other tasks. In the early 1930s she became a resident at Kingsley Hall community centre, London.

West, Albert (b.circa1880) Of peasant stock in Lincolnshire. He had a modest education and expressed his opinions in a down-to-earth manner. He went to South Africa in 1903 and ran a printing press with a European partner. That same year he met Gandhi in a vegetarian restaurant in Johannesburg. At Gandhi's request he took charge of printing *Indian Opinion* in Durban for £10 a month. He was the first to view Phoenix along with Gandhi. He printed *Indian Opinion* from Phoenix when they moved there on 24 December 1904 and had a monthly allowance of £3 like the others there. In June 1908 he married at Phoenix Ada Pywell from Leicester whose mother settled there also. In 1913 600 *satyagrahis* took refuge at Phoenix and he was arrested on 26

November for harbouring them. He was also reporting regularly to Gokhale in India. He edited *Indian Opinion* 1916-18 and managed the settlement until 1918. The Wests with their two children left Phoenix after 1918 as they found farming a struggle and settled in Durban where Albert had a printing press while Manilal took over the editorship of *Indian Opinion*. West kept up his interest in Indian affairs but the family moved to Britain in 1948. In 1963 he was invited by the Indian Government to visit India for 6 weeks where he visited places associated with Gandhi and wrote some reminiscences.

Winterbottom, Florence (d.1927) Gandhi met her in November 1906 when she was Corresponding Secretary of the Union of Ethical Societies. They met again on his next London visit and in July 1909 she invited Gandhi to hear Stanton Coit at the West London Ethical Church. The Ethical movement was one that appealed to Gandhi and he translated Salter's *Ethical Religion* into Gujarati. She introduced him to Ramsay MacDonald. Gandhi addressed the Union of Ethical Societies on 8 October 1909 on 'The Ethics of Passive Resistance' with Florence Winterbottom in the chair. She gave strong support to the Indian cause and corresponded frequently with Gandhi.

Bibliography

Ashe, Geoffrey *Gandhi: A Study in Revolution* Heinemann 1968.

Bacon, Josephine *The Illustrated Atlas of Jewish Civilisation* Quantum Books, London 1998.

Bartolf, Christian (Ed.) *The Breath of My Life* Correspondence of Mahatma Gandhi and Bart de Ligt on War and Peace Gandhi-Informations-Zentrum, Berlin 2000.

Berning, Gillian (Ed.) *Gandhi Letters: From Upper House to Lower House 1906-14* Local History Museum, Durban 1994.

Britton, Burnett *Gandhi Arrives in South Africa.* Greenleaf Books, Maine 1999.

Brown, Judith M. and Prozesky, Martin, Eds. *Gandhi and South Africa: Principles and Politics* University of Natal Press 1996.

Chatterjee, Margaret *Gandhi and His Jewish Friends* Macmillan 1992.

Chatterjee, Margaret *Gandhi and the Challenge of Religious Diversity* Promilla & Co., New Delhi 2005.

Copley, Antony *Gandhi Against the Tide* Basil Blackwell 1987, and Oxford India Paperbacks 1993.

Dhupelia-Mesthrie, Uma (Ed.) *Sita: Memoirs of Sita Gandhi* Durban Local History Museum 2003.

Dhupelia-Mesthrie, Uma *Gandhi's Prisoner ? The Life of Gandhi's Son Manilal* Kwela Books 2004

Doke, Joseph J. *Gandhi: A Patriot in South Africa.* G A Natesan & Co, Madras 1909 (reprinted by Government of India 1992).

Fogelman, Eva *Conscience and Courage : Rescuers of Jews During the Holcaust* Anchor Books 1994.

Gandhi, Arun and Sunanda *The Untold Story of Kasturba, Wife of Mahatma Gandhi* Jaico Publishing House, Mumbai 2000.

Gandhi, M. K. *The Story of My Experiments with Truth* Navajivan Publishing House, Ahmedabad 1927.

Gandhi, M. K. *Satyagraha in South Africa* Navajivan Publishing House, Ahmedabad 1928.

Gandhi, Prabhudas *My Childhood with Gandhiji* Navajivan Publishing House, Ahmedabad 1957.

Gandhi, Rajmohan *The Good Boatman: A Portrait of Gandhi* Penguin 1995

Green, Martin *Tolstoy and Gandhi: Men of Peace* Pennsylvania State University 1986.

Hunt, James D. *An American Looks at Gandhi: Essays in Satyagraha, Civil Rights and Peace* Promilla & Co. in association with Bibliophile South Asia, New Delhi & Chicago 2005.

Hunt, James D. *Gandhi and the Nonconformists: Encounters in South Africa* Promilla & Co, New Delhi 1986.

Hunt, James D. *Gandhi in London* Promilla & Co., New Delhi Revised Edition 1993.

Itzkin, Eric *Gandhi's Johannesburg: Birthplace of Satyagraha* Witwatersrand University Press, Johannesburg 2000.

Ligt, Bart de *The Conquest of Violence: an Essay on War and Revolution* Pluto Press 1989.

Nanda, B. R . *In Search of Gandhi* OUP 2002.

Nayar, Sushila *Mahatma Gandhi Vol IV Satyagraha at Work* Navajivan Publishing House, Ahmedabad 1989.

Payne, Robert *The Life and Death of Mahatma Gandhi* The Bodley Head 1969.

Parekh, Bhikhu *Colonialism, Tradition and Reform* Sage Publications 1999.

Polak, Millie Graham *Mr Gandhi: The Man* George Allen & Unwin, London 1931.

Polak, H. R. L., Brailsford, H. N., Pethick-Lawrence, F. W. *Mahatma Gandhi* Odhams Press, London 1949.

Powers, Roger S. '"But What About Hitler ?": Nonviolent Resistance Against Nazism' *Fellowship* May/June 1995.

Pyarelal *Mahatma Gandhi Volume III The Birth of Satyagraha* Navajivan Publishing House, Ahmedabad 1986.

Reddy, E. S. & Gandhi, Gopalkrishna, (Ed.) *Gandhi and South Africa 1914-1948* Navajivan 1993.

Saks, David Y. 'Right-Hand Man of the Mahatma: Hermann Kallenbach, Gandhi and Satyagraha.' *Jewish Affairs* Autumn 1998.

Sarid, Isa and Bartolf, Christian *Hermann Kallenbach: Mahatma Gandhi's Friend in South Africa* Gandhi-Informations-Zentrum, Berlin 1997.

Sharp, Gene *Gandhi as a Political Strategist* Porter Sargent, Boston 1979.

Shimoni, Gideon *Satyagraha, Gandhi and the Jews: A formative factor in India's policy towards Israel*. Jerusalem Papers on Peace Problems No. 22, Jerusalem 1977.

Swan, Maureen *Gandhi: The South African Experience* Ravan Press, Johannesburg 1985

Uppal, J. N. *Gandhi Ordained in Africa* Government of India 1995.

Weber, Thomas *Gandhi as Disciple and Mentor* Cambridge UP 2004

Wilcock, Evelyn *Pacifism and the Jews* Hawthorn Press, Stroud 1994.

Index

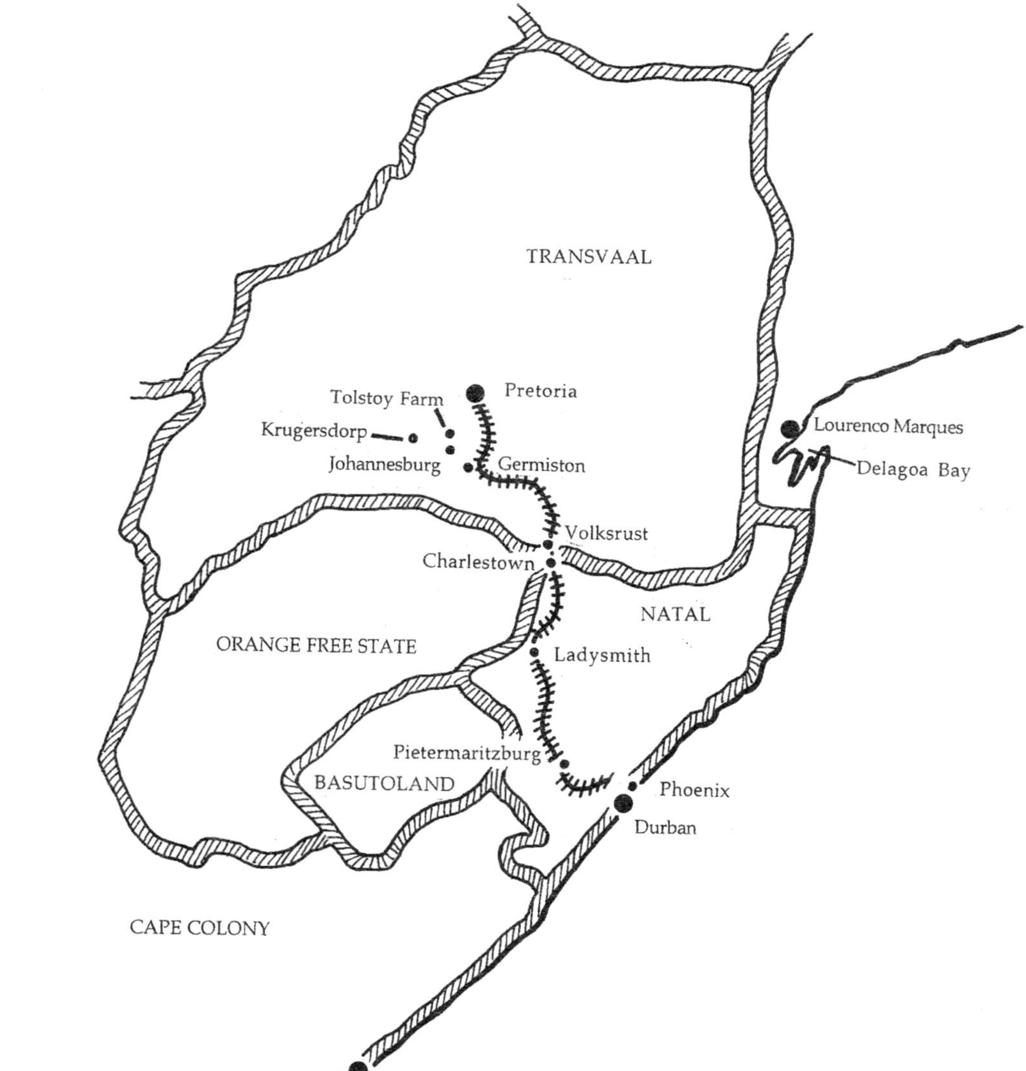
TRANSVAAL
Tolstoy Farm
Pretoria
Krugersdorp
Johannesburg
Germiston
Lourenco Marques
Delagoa Bay
Volksrust
Charlestown
NATAL
ORANGE FREE STATE
Ladysmith
Pietermaritzburg
BASUTOLAND
Phoenix
Durban
CAPE COLONY

Court in terms of Articles of Clerkship, copy wher whereof is annexed hereto marked "A".

2. That in reply to a letter addressed by the said M. K. Gandhi to the Secretary of the said Incorporated Law Society enquiring whether there was any legal objection to females taking up Articles of Clerkship to any Attorney the Secretary of the said Society replied in terms of letter of the 25th January 1909, that the articling of women is entirely without precedent in South Africa and was never contemplated by the Law, and, therefore, his Council would consider it their duty to refuse to register such Articles, copy of which letter is attached hereto marked "B".

3. That your Petitioner duly complied with the terms of Section 15, Ordinance 1 (Private) of 1905 and likewise duly deposited

with

Pages from the appeal to the Transvaal High Court against the Law Society's rejection of Schlesin's articleship with the said Secretary the prescribed fee.

4. That thereafter a further letter dated the 5th March 1909 was addressed by the Secretary of the said Society to the said M. K. Gandhi stating that his Council could not see its way to accept the Articles, and must refuse to register same, copy of which letter is attached hereto marked "C".

Wherefore your Petitioner prays that it may please this Honourable Court to grant an Order compelling the said Incorporated Law Society of the Transvaal to accept the said Articles of Clerkship for the purpose of registration, or that it may please this Honourable Court to grant such other or further relief as may seem meet in the premises, together with costs of this Application.

And your Petitioner as in duty bound will ever pray.

Sonja Schlesin.
Isidor Schlesin